Tax Guide 201

CAPITAL
GAINS &
LOSSES

by

Holmes F. Crouch
Tax Specialist

Published by

Allyear Tax Guides

**20484 Glen Brae Drive
Saratoga, CA 95070**

ISBN 0944817777

LCCN 2006920393

Printed in U.S.A.

Series 200
Investors & Businesses

Tax Guide 201

CAPITAL GAINS & LOSSES

For other titles in print, see page 224.

ii

The author: **Holmes F. Crouch**
For more about the author, see page 221.

PREFACE

If you are a knowledge-seeking **taxpayer** looking for information, this book can be helpful to you. It is designed to be read — from cover to cover — in about eight hours. Or, it can be "skim-read" in about 30 minutes.

Either way, you are treated to **tax knowledge** . . . *beyond the ordinary*. The "beyond" is that which cannot be found in IRS publications, the IRS web site, IRS e-file instructions, or tax software programs.

Taxpayers have different levels of interest in a selected subject. For this reason, this book starts with introductory fundamentals and progresses onward. You can verify the progression by chapter and section in the table of contents. In the text, "applicable law" is quoted in pertinent part. Key phrases and key tax forms are emphasized. Real-life examples are given . . . in down-to-earth style.

This book has 12 chapters. This number provides depth without cross-subject rambling. Each chapter starts with a head summary of meaningful information.

To aid in your skim-reading, informative diagrams and tables are placed strategically throughout the text. By leafing through page by page, reading the summaries and section headings, and glancing at the diagrams and tables, you can get a good handle on the matters covered.

Effort has been made to update and incorporate all of the latest tax law changes that are *significant* to the title subject. However, "beyond the ordinary" does not encompass every conceivable variant of fact and law that might give rise to protracted dispute and litigation. Consequently, if a particular statement or paragraph is crucial to your own specific case, you are urged to seek professional counseling. Otherwise, the information presented is general and is designed for a broad range of reader interests.

The Author

INTRODUCTION

Your broker reports one of your stock sales to the IRS on Form 1099-B: *Proceeds from Broker Transactions*. He reports that you sold X-number of shares in the ABC Corporation for which you received $26,256 in gross proceeds. This was in error. The correct amount should have been $16,256 (a $10,000 "typo" by your broker). How do you correct this error?

☐ Do nothing ☐ Notify broker ☐ Notify broker 2nd time

☐ Correct it on your own tax return.

The answer is: (1) Notify your broker, and then (2) Correct it on your tax return when preparing *Schedule D (Form 1040)*.

How do you do this? Well, that's what our Chapter 3: **Matching Payer Reportings**, is all about.

We have other chapters that address the preparatory "details" of Schedule D: *Capital Gains and Losses*. The schedule accommodates the results of virtually every capital asset disposition that an *individual* investor takes part in. Capital losses as well as gains are reported. The entry reportings are made by you (or by your tax preparer) in three functional groupings: (1) direct, (2) indirect, and (3) pass-through.

The direct entries are those computations you make directly on Schedule D based on broker-supplied information on Forms 1099-B, 1099-DIV, and 1099-S. The indirect entries are those transferred onto Schedule D from self-prepared "associated forms" such as: Forms 2439 (undistributed gains), 4684 (casualties and thefts), 4797 (business property sales), 6252 (installment sales), 6781 (straddles and options), and 8824 (like-kind exchanges). The pass-through entries are those which you extract from Schedules K-1 prepared by partnerships, S corporations, estates, and trusts.

All of this entry detail has to be segregated, formulated, subtotaled, and gain/loss netted. Hopefully, the result is a net long-term capital gain. If so, the 15% tax rate will dominate your subsequent computations. If, instead, there is a net capital loss, the 15% rate (of course) will not apply. In such case, loss limitation and loss carryover rules apply.

Once you have derived net long-term capital gain, you enter a special world of preferential tax treatment. We call this the "15% tax rate" world. This 15% rate applies not only to net long-term capital gain (assets held more than one year), but also to capital gain distributions from mutual funds and to qualified dividends from public corporations. Qualified dividends are from common stock that is held for at least 61 days within a 121-day period that begins 60 days before the ex-dividend date.

We use the term "15% tax rate" because it is not graduated as in the case of ordinary income rates (from 10% to 35%). The 15% capital gains tax is not subject to the add-on of Social Security and Medicare tax (7.65% for employees and 15.3% for self-employeds), nor is it subject to the Alternative Minimum Tax at its rates of 26% and 28%.

The 15% rate cuts a wide swath across the spectrum of transactional gains by successful investors. Yes, there is one lower rate of 5% (for those in the 10% ordinary income bracket) and two higher rates for the disposition of special assets. There is a 25% rate when depreciable real property used in a trade or business is sold. There is also a 28% rate for realized gain on collectibles (art, coins, antiques, etc.), and on the sale of qualified small business stock. Fortunately, very few individual investors have to deal with the 25% and 28% gain rates. For those who do, there are (rather complicated) tax worksheets and software programs available. All others need to focus only on the 15% rate. From this one low tax rate, great power, privilege, and wealth can be your reward. To achieve this reward, however, your close personal attention to proper tax accounting and recordkeeping are required.

On point is one very important matter. This is reconstructing your provable *cost or other basis* in each asset sold. Your "basis money" is recoverable tax free. Consequently, it is our intention to keep you on your toes with respect to the many subtleties in the capital gain and capital loss tax rules. When you are through reading this book, you'll know better what the fine points are. Your brokers, friends, and mentors may not.

CONTENTS

1

SCHEDULE D (1040) OVERVIEW

> The Format And Methodology Of Schedule D Are Dominated By The IRS's Computer Matching Of Sales Price Amounts Reported To It By Payers, Versus Those Amounts You Report. The "Schedule" Consists Of 15 Entry Lines Arranged Into "Line Pairs" Such As: 1/8, 2/9, 3/10, 4/11, 5/12, 6/14, And 7/15. Except For Line 13 (Capital Gain Distributions), The Line Pairs Consist Of Short-Term (More Than One Year) And Long-Term Holdings. Otherwise, The Pairs Distinguish Between Different Investors And Their Chosen Activities. For Pairs 1/8 And 2/9, There Are 6 Entry Columns, Of Which Column (f): GAIN Or <LOSS> Is Most Tax Significant.

By far the most important single tax form for every investor is **Schedule D (Form 1040)**. It is titled: *Capital Gains and Losses.* The parenthetical association with "Form 1040" is, of course, your *U.S. Individual Income Tax Return* for the taxable year at issue. There is also a Schedule D (1041) for trusts, Schedule D (1065) for partnerships, and Schedule D (1120) for corporations. We are addressing herein exclusively, Schedule D (**1040**) . . . and its continuation Schedules D-1.

Below the official title to Schedule D (1040), there are three little headnotes which say:

▸ Attach to Form 1040.
▸ See Instructions for Schedule D.
▸ Use Schedule D-1 for additional transactions.

On page 1 of Form 1040, there is a line which reads:

Capital gain or <loss>. Attach Schedule D if required.

The Schedule D title term "gains and losses" refers to the **separate listing** of the gain or loss for each transaction . . . plus other transactions entered on associated forms which also attach to Form 1040. The title term also includes the summarizing and netting of all gains and losses for the entire year. The Schedule D "bottom line" therefore is *either* (a) a net capital gain, **or** (b) a net capital loss. It is "or": **not** "and." One or the other is transferred onto Form 1040. There is only one such entry line, whether or not you attach Schedule D.

In this introductory chapter, we want to tell you those things about Schedule D that your broker, financial adviser, or mentor may not have passed on to you. Schedule D has a methodology and life of its own. Said life is not self-evident in your ordinary course of investment affairs, nor is it readily apparent in the tax software that you may procure. There are certain "vital signs" that you need to know about, but we cannot convey these signs to you without discussing the various parts, columns, line numbers, line captions, and line instructions that are loaded onto Schedule D. Therefore, we are going to simply "overview" Schedule D in this chapter, and cover in subsequent chapters the details for your mastering it. Our experience has been that the IRS does not examine Schedule D as carefully as it might, if your "sales price" entries survive its electronic processing with no mismatchings.

The Scheme of Things

We have indicated above that Schedule D attaches to your Form 1040 . . . if required. What does "if required" mean?

It means that, if you have made any reportable capital gain/loss transaction for the year, you must show the computed gain or loss for each transaction on Schedule D. A "reportable" transaction is where you are the owner of an asset and you yourself directed its disposition. You have to report the date of its disposition and its selling price. You also have to report its date of acquisition and its cost or other basis when acquired, plus improvements (if any) prior to its being sold.

Schedule D is also required when you have includible transactions. An "includible" transaction is where you do not participate directly in the transactional decisions. You are a shareholder in a mutual fund or S corporation, a partner in a partnership, or a beneficiary of an estate or trust. The decisions are made by some manager, and your distributive share of any gains or losses is passed through to you.

If you are a distributee (recipient) of capital gains from a mutual fund or real estate investment trust, and have no other transactional gains or losses to report, no Schedule D is required. In this case, you check a box ☒ on the capital gain/loss line on Form 1040 and enter the total distributions there.

On the other hand, if you have qualified dividends (we mentioned them in our Introduction), you enter the total amount on Form 1040 **and** on Schedule D. Although these are stock dividends, because they are "qualified," they are treated as long-term capital gain. All of which means that there is another tax form (1099-DIV) which is associated with Schedule D and with Form 1040, but not attached to either.

Confusing? Well, perhaps. It perhaps is so because Schedule D is a quite formidable form that accommodates many different investor activities. To try to discuss each variant activity at this moment would be too overwhelming. Instead, we present in Figure 1.1 a block diagram of the scheme of things surrounding Schedule D. We suggest that you glance at this figure for a moment. After you do so, we'll point out a few features to orient you for the chapters which follow

First off, note in Figure 1.1 that page 2 of Form 1040 and of Schedule D are functionally similar: *Summary & Tax Computation*. These descriptive words do not appear on the official forms. Particularly note that there are five computational worksheets that feed into page 2 of Schedule D. We are nowhere near ready to tell you about the tax computational aspects therewith. Hence, we suspend all such matters until we get to Chapter 12: Computing Related Tax (re Schedule D).

Next, note in Figure 1.1 the three boxes (A, B, and C) that feed onto page 1 of Schedule D. All three will be touched on in

Chapter 3: Matching Payer Reportings. All broker/payer reportings are made on Forms 1099, otherwise known as: *Information returns*. Box A will be addressed in Chapter 6: Direct Entry Transactions, using applicable 1099s. Box B will be addressed in Chapter 8: Indirect Gain/Loss Entries. These entries require separate forms which attach to Schedule D. Box C will be addressed in Chapter 9: Gain/Loss from Schedule(s) K-1, for pass-through entities.

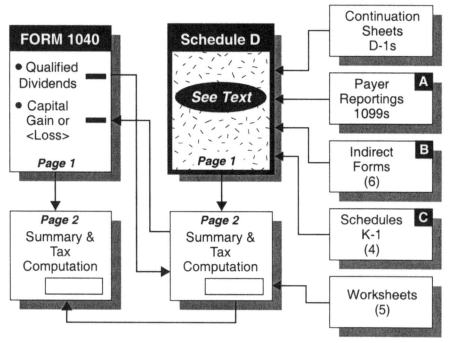

Fig. 1.1 - The "Scheme" of Schedule D (1040) and Its Associated Forms

And, finally, note in Figure 1.1 the new-kid-on-the-block: *Qualified dividends*. These dividends are entered from Form 1099-DIV onto page 1 of Form 1040. From here the amount is transferred to page 2 of Schedule D where it settles in with the tax mix that goes back to page 2 of Form 1040. We devote all of Chapter 11 (Qualified Dividends) to this one item alone.

Are you ready now for a closer examination of Schedule D (1040) before attaching it to your Form 1040?

The Year 2005 Form

For years since 1969 (the first "Tax Reform Act" since the origin of U.S. income tax), capital gains have enjoyed preferential tax treatment. The rationale for so was — as it is to this day — to encourage investors to participate in productive enterprises that would grow the national economy. The applicable tax rates, holding periods, and enterprise activities for preferential treatment varied considerably. This meant that the Schedule D format also varied from year to year. It appears now with the dominant focus currently on a 15% capital gains tax rate, and an asset holding period requirement of more than year, that the design and format of Schedule D (1040) has settled down. This is particularly true for its page 1: the front side. Accordingly, the year 2005 format, we think, is about "it" for a reasonable period of years to come.

Page 1 of Schedule D (1040) consists of two parts, namely:

Part I. Short-Term Capital Gains and Losses
— Assets Held One Year or Less

Part II. Long-Term Capital Gains and Losses
— Assets Held More Than One Year

Note the underlying difference between these two parts: short-term vs. long-term. Short-term gains get no preferential treatment, whatsoever, with respect to tax rates. Such gains are treated as ordinary income. Only *long-term* capital gains enjoy lower than ordinary tax rates.

Part I (short-term) consists of seven lines, whereas Part II (long-term) consists of eight lines (total 15). The extra line in Part II addresses *Capital gain distributions* only. In fact, this is the official caption for that line. If these distributions come from a stock/bond mutual fund and/or from a real estate investment trust, who really knows what the underlying asset holding period was? Nevertheless, Congress wanted to extend preferential treatment to such endeavors.

The capital gain distribution line is designated as "line 13" on Schedule D, Part II. Ordinarily, we are reluctant to cite the official line numbers and captions on a tax form. This is because they tend to change from year to year. This, however, has not been the case recently for Parts I and II of Schedule D. Because of their instructional and comprehensional value, we'll cite all 15 lines for you. We have already cited line 13. This leaves us 14 lines to go.

Don't worry. We'll not bore you. We'll pair the lines up into "short/long" so that there are really only seven lines. We demonstrate this pairing in Figure 1.2. It is the functional substance of the seven lines that we want to address in this chapter: not the details. We have tried to abbreviate the substance of each line in the right-hand column of Figure 1.2.

Page 1	SCHEDULE D (FORM 1040)	Year
Line Numbers		
Short Term	Long Term	**THE SUBJECT OF FOCUS**
1	8	Basic transactional entries
2	9	Totals from "Continuation Sheets"
3	10	Total sales price amounts
4	11	Gain/Loss from 6 "associated" forms
5	12	Gain/Loss from 4 K-1 entities
////	13	Capital Gain distributions
6	14	Capital loss carryovers
7	15	Net gain or <loss> for year

Fig. 1.2 - The Functional Pairing of Lines on Schedule D

For the ordinary investor, lines 1/8 would probably get the lion's share of one's Schedule D attention. These are the direct gain/loss entry lines that we have alluded to previously. These are the most used and most hands-on entry lines by those who direct their own acquisition and disposition transactional events. If you do your homework assiduously, and keep good transactional records, your self-discipline on these two lines (1 and 8) will serve you well for all other lines on Schedule D as well as with its various "associated forms." We urge you, therefore, to master lines 1 and 8.

The 6 Columnar Headings

To master the operative importance of lines 1 and 8, you must read and comprehend the columnar headings. There are six such columns which are designated sequentially as: column (a) through column (f). On the face of Schedule D only, lines 1 and 8 have six columns for entry purposes. With the exception of line 2/9 (which has two columns) and line 3/10 (which has column (d) only), all other lines have just one column, namely: column (f). That is, of the total of 15 lines on Schedule D, nine involve column (f) only.

What are the six columnar headings? They are as follows—

Col. (a) — *Description of property*
Col. (b) — *Date acquired*
Col. (c) — *Date sold*
Col. (d) — *Sales price*
Col. (e) — *Cost or other basis*
Col. (f) — ***Gain or <loss>***

Below each of these primary captions, there are small-print instructions. They are more or less self-explanatory. Columns (b) and (c) regarding dates require that each entry be designated by its *month*, *day*, and *year*. This is for holding period reasons. The holding period begins the **day after** an asset is acquired and ends on the date of sale. Being short just one day can mean the difference between a 35% tax rate (short-term) and a 15% tax rate (long-term). The date "sold" in column (c) means the date that you disposed of (gave up ownership to) the asset described in column (a) with abbreviated specificity.

The small print sublines in columns (d) [sales price] and (e) [cost or other basis] say— *See instructions.* We'll go into more instructional detail in Chapters 3, 4, 5, and 6 herein. The IRS focuses on the "sales price" reported by your broker.

The small print subline in column (f) says—

Subtract (e) from (d).

This is quite straightforward and requires no further computational explanation on our part. The result is: ***Gain or <Loss>***. The column (f) heading is officially in bold print; no other columns are so. Other columns have parenthesized instructions in small print.

The term "loss" in column (f) is officially designated in parentheses ( ). But we prefer the use of brackets < > instead. In our view, when dealing with arithmetical positive and negative amounts, the use of brackets < > provides more computational focus. Brackets < > also avoid confusion with text material which uses parentheses ( ). By the way, a zero is indicated by -0-. The front and back dashes make it clear that no other digit than zero is involved. We suppose you could enter the word "zero," but it is doubtful that the IRS's matching computer could read it.

Having breezed you through the above, we present in Figure 1.3 a simplified overview of the Schedule D format: Parts I and II thereof. Note that no line numbers are shown: just the columnar designation. We simply want you to get the functional drift of the kind of entries required. We particularly want you to note that the dominant column there is (f): **Gain or <loss>**. It runs through all lines except one, namely: *Total Sales Price Amounts*. We'll get to the reason for this in a moment. In the meantime, we need to tell you about certain "continuation" sheets.

Continuation Schedule(s) D-1

At the very beginning of this chapter, we pointed out that there were certain headnotes below the official title to Schedule D. One of these headnotes made reference to a "Schedule D-1." The more official headnote instruction (on Schedule D) reads—

Use Schedule D-1 to list additional transactions for lines 1 and 8.

Line 1 on Schedule D-1 accommodates short-term direct transactional entries, whereas line 8 accommodates long-term transactions. There is a direct correlation between lines 1 and 8 on Schedule D with the same lines on Schedule D-1. The six columns on D and D-1 correlate directly as well. The reason for this correlation is that Schedule D-1 is a continuation sheet for Schedule D.

Schedule D-1 is officially titled and subtitled as follows—

Part I	ASSETS HELD ONE YEAR OR LESS				
(a)	(b)	(c)	(d)	(e)	(f) Gain <Loss>
From Schedules D-1				///////	
Total Sales Price Amounts				///////	///////
Indirect Entry Forms (4)					
From K-1 Entities					
Capital Loss Carryover					
Net Short-Term Gain or <Loss> ▶					

Part II	ASSETS HELD MORE THAN ONE YEAR				
(a)	(b)	(c)	(d)	(e)	(f) Gain <Loss>
From Schedules D-1				///////	
Total Sales Price Amounts				///////	///////
Indirect Entry Forms (6)					
From K-1 Entities					
Capital Loss Carryover					
Capital Gain Distributions					
					///////
Net Long-Term Gain or <Loss> ▶					

Fig. 1.3 - Page 1 of Schedule D (1040) Simplified

Continuation Sheet for Schedule D (Form 1040)

▶ *Attach to Schedule D to list additional transactions for lines 1 and 8*

What we haven't told you previously is that lines 1 and 8 of Schedule D each consists of only five unnumbered blank lines (with six columns). If you have more than five entry transactions (in either Part I or Part II), what do you do? It is not uncommon for some active investors to execute 100 or more transactions in a given year. Where do they report greater than five transactions?

Here's where the wisdom and flexibility of Schedule D-1 shines forth. Part I (short-term) is one full side of the page; Part II (long-term) is the reverse full side. The Part I page is **line 1**; the Part II page is **line 8**. Whereas Schedule D lines 1/8 accept only five transactions, Schedule D-1 lines 1/8 accept up to 24 transactions!

With one Schedule D-1, an investor could directly enter into either Part I or Part II a total of 29 transactions (24 + 5). But what if he engaged in 125 transactions for the year? How many Schedules D-1 would he need?

Answer: Five Schedules D-1 (5 x 24 = 120 transactions), plus five on Schedule D itself.

Since all Schedules D-1 are printed exactly alike, how would you distinguish between them, if you had more than one?

Simple. In the upper right-hand corner of each D-1, hand print #1, #2, . . . #5 sequentially. Do this on the Part I side unless you have absolutely no short-term transactions. If no short-terms, use the Part II side. There is just one precaution to keep in mind. At the very bottom of each D-1, there's a **Totals** line which reads—

Part I, **line 2** —*Add the amounts in **column (d)** [sales price]. Combine the amounts in **column (f)** [Gain or <loss>]. Enter here and on Schedule D, line 2.*

Similarly, for Part II, line 9. Instead of entering the totals on #1, #2, #3, and #4, you hand-print the word "**continued**" in lieu of the totals in each of the columns (d) and (f). You then enter the grand total for all D-1s on the #5 D-1, and follow the line 2 and line 9 instructions therewith. You are directed, respectively, onto the corresponding lines 2 and 9 on Schedule D.

Line 2 of Schedule D reads—

Enter your short-term totals, if any, from Schedule D-1, line 2.

Similarly, line 9 on Schedule D reads—

Enter your long-term totals, if any, from Schedule D-1, line 9.

We remind you that only two short-term totals and two long-term totals are transferred from Schedule D-1 to Schedule D. These are columns (d) [sales price] and (f) [gain or <loss>]. No column (e) [cost or other basis] information is transferred. This is because there is no way the IRS can computer match your cost information without a direct request for documentation from you.

Nevertheless, there is a basic and fundamental message in the Schedule(s) D-1 enablement. Each and every independent buy/sell type of transaction must be fully and faithfully reported on lines 1/8 of Schedule D and, as necessary, on lines 1/8 of the Schedule(s) D-1. You cannot aggregate the transactions (bunch several together) for your own convenience. If you do so, you'll be alarmed at what the IRS's computer-matching facility will do. We'll give you a hint after we apprise you of the single-column role of lines 3 and 10.

Sales Price Amounts

Back in Figure 1.2 we indicated that lines 3 and 10 were "sales price amounts." Each line is a one-column entry, namely in column (d). Each entry is the total of all sales prices — more accurately: *gross proceeds* — of all transactions individually reported on lines 1/8 and 2/9. The Part I (short-term) grand total is separately displayed from the Part II (long-term) grand total. These two totals have no bearing whatsoever on the Schedule D tax computation process. So why are these two totals displayed?

To help you visualize better what we are getting at, we present Figure 1.4. Note our purposeful emphasis on each "IRS FOCUS." Such emphasis does not appear on an official Schedule D.

The two sales price totals enable the IRS to cross check what you report on your Schedules D and D-1 with that which all of your payers report to the IRS. The payer reportings are those electronically filed on IRS **Form 1099-B**. This form is titled: ***Proceeds from Broker and Barter Exchange Transactions***. We'll tell you more about Form 1099-B in Chapter 3: Matching Payer Reportings. There are also other gross proceeds reportings that we'll touch on.

Here's how the computer-matching scheme generally works. Let's say that your Part II total sales price amount is $152,000.

Let's say that all of your payers report a total of $188,000. This is an electronic-matching discrepancy of $36,000 (188,000 — 152,000). That is, you *underreported* one or more transactions to this extent. What does the IRS do? Answer: It assesses you additional tax on $36,000. The IRS taxes you at ordinary income rates: **not** capital gain rates. At the same time, the IRS sends you a Notice of the discrepancy and invites your corrective comment, if you so wish.

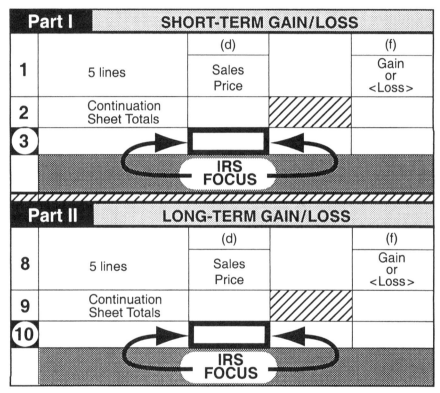

Fig. 1.4 - The Line Numbered "Bull's Eyes" in Parts I and II

On the other hand, if your Schedule D/D-1 total sales price amounts are $188,000 and the 1099-B payers report a total of $152,000, no action is taken by the IRS.

The IRS's position is that it is up to you to report correctly. The IRS is not required to computer-match every individual transaction you make. If, in the aggregate, you underreport, you pay additional ordinary tax. The tax presumption is that the payer — being a 3rd party unrelated to you — is correct. If you believe the payer is not correct, you have to take it up with the payer: not with the IRS.

If you overreport, you self-pay more capital gain tax than you need to. If you carelessly overpay your tax, that's your fault: not the IRS's. Do you understand the reasoning behind this message? You are provided the opportunity to report matters correctly on your own. You cannot expect the IRS to read your mind, nor can you expect it to contact payers individually on your behalf.

Subsequent Paired Lines

Next in our line count, there are three sets of paired lines that we should at least touch on. They are lines 4/11, 5/12, and 6/14. Earlier, we described line 13: *Capital gains distributions.* Since these gains are Congressionally mandated to be treated as long-term, there is no counterpart short-term line. Hence, instead of a paired line 6/13, it is 6/14.

Because of the complexity of these three paired lines, and also because we do not want to distract you from the importance of computer matching on lines 1/8, 2/9, and 3/10, we'll cite only their captions at this point. The captions alone will give you a foretaste of what is coming up in later chapters.

The line pair 4/11 reads precisely as—

Line 4 — *Short-term gain from Form 6252 and short-term gain or <loss> from Forms 4684, 6781, and 8824.*

Line 11 — *Gain from Form 4797, Part I; long-term gain from Forms 2439 and 6252; and long-term gain or <loss> from Forms 4684, 6781, and 8824.*

Altogether, six different Schedule D "associated" forms may be involved. Instead of cramming in here a hasty explanation of these indirect entry forms, isn't it better that we put them aside until Chapter 8: Indirect Gain/Loss Entries?

The next line pair 5/12 reads as follows:

Line 5 — *Net short-term gain or <loss> from partnerships, S corporations, estates, and trusts from Schedule(s) K-1.*

Line 12 — *Net long-term gain or <loss> from partnerships, S corporations, estates, and trusts from Schedule(s) K-1.*

Schedule(s) K-1? We really have to explain these to you. To do so properly, we have reserved Chapter 9 for this purpose: Gain/Loss from Schedule(s) K-1.

The last of the above-mentioned three line pairs is line 6/14. Each line reads basically as—

Line 6 — *Short-term capital loss carryover. Enter the amount, if any, from* . . . [another form].

Line 14 — *Long-term capital loss carryover. Enter the amount, if any, from* . . . [the same "other form" as in line 6].

The use of *net* capital losses for a given year is limited to <$3,000>. Losses in excess of this amount are carried over to successive years until used. There is more to it than this. That's why we have Chapter 10 much later: Capital Loss Treatment.

Overall, there is a well thought out methodology to Schedule D. This methodology is seldom self-evident to anxious taxpayers when preparing their Schedules D for the taxable year. Each of the different line pairs attempts to accommodate different investors with different degrees of activity and sophistication. In this respect, for summary purposes of this chapter, we invite your glance at Figure 1.5. Although we show what appears to be one bottom line, actually there are two. Having two bottom lines is probably the most distinguishing feature of Schedule D (1040).

Two Separate Bottom Lines

More specifically, page 1 of Schedule D has two bottom lines. (There is a page 2 which we haven't come to yet.) **Line 7** on page 1 is the bottom line for Part I (short-term); **line 15** is the bottom line for Part II (long-term). Each is separate and distinct from the other. There are tax treatment reasons for this. We defer discussion of the Part I/Part II tax treatments until much later. Meanwhile, let us describe the two bottom lines and the significance of each.

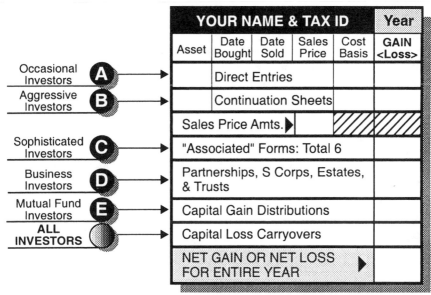

Fig. 1.5 - The "Accommodation" of Different Investors on Schedule D (1040)

The precise wording of each of the two bottom lines is this—

Line 7 — *Net short-term capital gain or <loss>.*
Combine lines 1 through 6 in column (f).
Line 15 — *Net long-term capital gain or <loss>.*
Combine lines 8 through 14 in column (f). Then
go to . . . [page 2 of Schedule D].

What is the caption for column (f); do you recall? It is—

Gain or <Loss>. *Subtract (e) from (d).*

Except for lines 3/10 — the IRS's computer matching focus: *Total sales price amounts* — column (f) runs from line 1 all the way down to line 15. We illustrated this back in Figure 1.3, where line 3 was cross-hatched across columns (e) and (f), and similarly for line 10.

What is the caption for column (d)? Answer: *Sales price.* Sales price? Isn't this what the IRS gets electronic information on from your payers? Yes, it is.

What is the caption for column (e)? Answer: *Cost or other basis (see the instructions).*

Cost or other basis? Where does that information come from? It comes from **your own records**. The IRS does not track this information for you. Nor is your broker or other agent required to do so. In some cases, your financial counselor will assist you if he/she handles all of your transactions for the year at issue. Otherwise, you are strictly on your own.

What if you have no cost or other basis records? You were just too busy making your millions. Tough! The IRS asserts that your tax basis is zero. In such case your sales price for each no-records transaction is all gain. It is taxable gain even though, in fact, you may have a total loss. We'll try to instruct you against this possibility, after presenting more foundational background on investor characteristics.

There is also a Part III (on page 2) of Schedule D. That page is officially titled: **Summary**. This title alone should be your hint that the two bottom lines on page 1 are synthesized in some manner to produce only one tax. Indeed, such is the sole purpose of Part III. There is much more you need to know before we get to the summary aspects of Schedule D.

2

HOW "INVESTOR" TAX DEFINED

> An Investor Is One Who Advances Money To Acquire A Capital Asset In Which He Exercises Primarily A Passive (NONLIVELIHOOD) Role. Upon Sale Or Exchange, If Capital Gain, He Pays Tax At Lower Rates. If Capital Loss, He Faces Tax Limitations. Either Way, He Pays No Social Security/Medicare Tax On The Gross Proceeds. In Contrast, An Entrepreneur Engages In A Trade Or Business For Livelihood Purposes. If He Profits, He Pays TWO TAXES: Ordinary Income And Social Security/Medicare. If He Loses, All Losses Are Tax Recognized. Investors Who Do Active Trading (Daily Or Otherwise) Are NOT Entrepreneurs.

An "investor"? What's so special about being an investor? Doesn't everyone know what an investor is? An investor is someone who puts money into an investment. What kind of investment? Several kinds: stocks, bonds, securities, commodities, real estate, retail businesses, mining ventures, manufacturing enterprises, communication facilities, information technology . . . and so on.

In the most general sense, one thinks of an investor as anyone who puts up money to make money. Making money is fine. But what happens if one loses money? The tax treatment of making money and losing money is what distinguishes an investor from other persons who engage in investment-type entrepreneurial activities. There is a definite tax line between who is an investor and who is an entrepreneur.

When an investor makes money, he gets preferential tax treatment in the form of lower capital gains rates. We discussed these lower rates quite prominently in our Introduction. On the other hand, if an investor loses money, he is subjected to detrimental limitations. If he net loses $10,000, for example, he can only use $3,000 of the loss for that year. He can carry over the remaining $7,000 loss at the rate of $3,000 per year thereafter. We'll discuss the treatment of investor capital losses in Chapter 10.

In contrast, an entrepreneur gets ordinary income treatment when he makes money. In addition to nonpreferential rates, he also pays social security and medicare tax on his net income. If he loses money, however, say the same $10,000 as above, the full $10,000 is tax recognized in the year of the loss. In other words, losses are more beneficial to an entrepreneur than to an investor.

Sometimes a taxpayer wants it both ways. When he makes money, he wants to be treated as an investor. When he loses money, he wants to be treated as an entrepreneur. Having it both ways won't work. The IRS will see to this . . . and so will the courts, in contested cases. We cite two such cases (*F.R. Mayer* and *R.W. Steffler*) on page 2-12 herein.

In this chapter, therefore, we want to present the tax lines of distinction between an investor and an entrepreneur. As a hint in this regard, one's extent of personal participation in making money is a key factor. The tax laws on this point are not crystal clear, nor are the many court decisions that have been rendered thereon. Nevertheless, there are certain guidelines you can depend on for making your choice. Since the book is for investors — NOT entrepreneurs — we naturally want to acquaint you with all of the favorable features of an investor that we can.

Capital Asset Defined

An investor invests money in a capital asset. So, too, can an entrepreneur. And thus we have the beginning of why an investor and entrepreneur are often misdiagnosed as one and the same. They are not. But you wouldn't know this explicitly from the tax definition of a capital asset.

Section 1221 of the Internal Revenue Code is titled: *Capital Asset Defined*. Its leadoff sentence reads—

*The term "capital asset" means property held by the taxpayer (**whether or not** connected with his trade or business), but does not include . . .* [Emphasis added.]

We stop the citation (temporarily) at this point because we want you to focus on the term "whether or not." If you think about it for a moment, the "whether or not" applies to two generic types of taxpayers: investors **and** entrepreneurs. What's the difference? They both can acquire capital assets.

The difference is that, when an investor acquires a capital asset, it is not used in connection with his trade or business, occupation, or livelihood activities. An entrepreneur, on the other hand, uses — or may use — the capital asset in connection with his livelihood trade or business. An entrepreneur may "invest" money to buy inventory (for sale to customers), a structure (shop or warehouse), and/or machinery for farming or mining. The term "trade or business" is a tax icon of long standing. It applies to any activity in which one generates ordinary income for livelihood purposes.

Now, to continue with Section 1221. The term "capital asset" *. . . **does not include**—*

(1) Stock in trade of the taxpayer or other property of a kind which would properly be included in inventory of the taxpayer if on hand at the close of the taxable year, or property held by the taxpayer for sale to customers in the ordinary course of his trade or business;

(2) Property, used in his trade or business, of a character which is subject to the allowance for depreciation . . ., or real property used in his trade or business;

(3) A copyright, a literary, musical, or artistic composition, a letter or memorandum, or similar property, held by a taxpayer whose personal efforts created such property [or] *for whom such property was prepared or produced;*

(4) Accounts or notes receivable acquired in the ordinary course of trade or business for services rendered or from the sale of property described in paragraph (1).

Have you spotted the common thread that distinguishes noncapital assets from capital assets? The common thread is: "connected with," "held by," "used in," "created for," or "in the ordinary course of" . . . one's trade or business. In other words, it is the relationship of an asset to one's trade or business (livelihood activities) that characterizes it as a *noncapital* asset. It is "noncapital" in the sense that it is owner-used for productive purposes in which the owner contributes his personal services. If there is no personal service relationship, you have a capital asset.

In practice, this distinction makes sense. A pure investor should not depend on his investment results for livelihood purposes. The obvious reason is that he could lose money as well as make it. A capital asset can increase or decrease in value when sold or exchanged. Upon such sale or exchange, the former asset holder (investor) gets capital gain treatment . . . or capital loss treatment. The tax treatment differs for an entrepreneur.

Passivity: The Main Key

There is one key, basic characteristic that distinguishes an investor from all other taxpayers, including entrepreneurs. He plays a purely passive role in the management of capital assets. Any active role therewith is performed solely by market forces.

An investor makes the decision to acquire a capital asset. Once he does so, he sits back and observes the market fluctuations in the value of that asset. Time passes. As it does, an investor may take, or be given, "snapshots" of the condition of his asset. Other than occasional observations, he does not significantly participate in its day-to-day happenings. Someone else, or some entity, does. Then, at some later point in time, an investor decides to sell or otherwise dispose of his asset.

The passivity role of an investor does not mean that he puts up his money then forgets about it. It simply means that he does not participate actively in the market place in a direct (trade or business) manner. That is, he exercises no direct influence on the change in value of his asset with time. He may repair and maintain his asset, or even improve it, but otherwise he is purely on the sidelines. He hardly turns a hand to influence its gain or loss. An exception would be certain real estate needing renovations.

In essence, then, an investor puts money into an asset, watches it gain or lose, and decides when to sell/dispose of that asset. His active attention consists of three distinct phases, namely:

Phase I — The mental decision to buy
Phase II — The emotional observation over time
Phase III — The mental decision to sell

Using Figure 2.1 as a background reference, let us give a simple example of the passivity role of an investor. Take a one ounce gold coin.

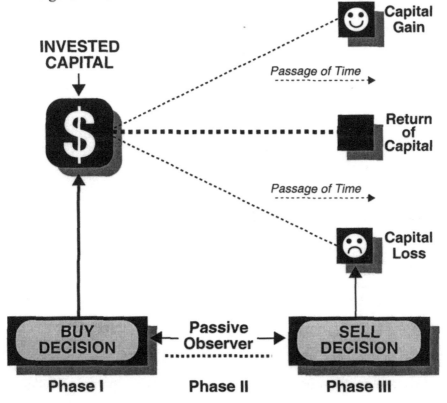

Fig. 2.1 - Passivity: The Primary Characteristic of an Investor

A gold coin is a pure — and sterile — investment asset. It does not earn income; it does not change in size and shape. It does not tarnish and it does not wear out on its own. It cannot be eaten or otherwise consumed in productive enterprise. Once formed it stays fixed (even over thousands of years) until purposely destroyed by melting it down.

An investor buys a gold coin and puts it in his dresser drawer. Certainly, he did some research on where to buy and on what type of coin to buy. But this is a decision-making process of his own. In the dresser drawer, the coin is dormant. The investor himself can do nothing to influence the value of the coin with the passage of time. Market forces entirely beyond his control influence the coin's value while it is being held as an investment.

Sometime later, the investor takes his coin out of the drawer, and sells it. Again, a mental decision is required to do this. Whether he gets more money back, or less money back than he paid, will depend on market factors over time. As to these market factors, the role of the coin investor was truly passive.

No Social Security Tax

Why is passivity so important to an investor?

Because if he makes a gain, gets his money back, or suffers a loss, there is no Social Security/Medicare tax to pay!

The Social Security/Medicare tax is the most inflexible tax of modern time. It starts with the very first dollar of *personal participation* income. It is a fixed percentage each year. It is not graduated in any way; it is truly a "flat tax." It applies to a specified "participation base" which may increase from year to year. Against the first and subsequent participation base dollars, there are no offsets for adjustments, deductions, and expenses. Politically, it is called a "contribution," but administratively it is called a "tax" (to make it compulsory). One is compelled to pay Social Security/Medicare tax on (virtually) every personal participation dollar that he makes.

Because of his passive role in the making or losing of dollars, an investor pays no Social Security/Medicare tax on his investment proceeds. For those assets towards which he takes on an active personal service role, he *does* pay the added tax. The Social Security/Medicare tax is a *second* tax on personal service income. Hence, passivity in connection with one's investment assets is the distinguishing feature that relieves one from such tax. There are, indeed, social wisdom and virtue in the "second tax."

The Social Security system is not a voluntary matter at all. If one is employed or self-employed, he is mandated to pay into the system. Because it is a contributions tax, it is referred to in the Internal Revenue Code as "other taxes."

For employees, Section 3101(a) of the IR Code applies. This section carries the official heading: *Old-Age, Survivors, and Disability Insurance*. Its introductory wording reads—

In addition to other taxes, there is hereby imposed on the income of every individual a tax equal to the [designated] *percentage of the wages . . . received by him with respect to employment.* [Emphasis added.]

For self-employeds, Section 1401(a) applies. This section carries the same official heading as Section 3101(a) above. The introductory wording of Section 1401(a) reads—

In addition to other taxes, there shall be imposed for each taxable year, on the self-employment income of every individual, a tax equal to the [designated] *percent of the amount of the self-employment income for such taxable year.*

If an investor becomes too active in his wheelings and dealings, day to day, he crosses the threshold into the domain of a self-employed participant (in the market place). When he does so, the Social Security/Medicare tax promptly applies. A true investor is neither employed in the business of making investments nor self-employed therein. His capital alone does the work.

"Trade or Business" Explained

To avoid paying Social Security/Medicare tax on investment proceeds, an investor must not be in a trade or business (with his invested money). What constitutes a trade or business, therefore, should be explained.

Basically, a trade or business is a pursuit carried on for livelihood via profit. That is, one engages in an activity on a regular basis to produce income and livelihood. To produce a livelihood, one needs to make a *profit, more or less regularly.* If no net profit is made in a reasonable span of time, one quits that pursuit and, perhaps, starts another. One's livelihood derives from the profits made: not from the losses incurred.

The pursuit of a livelihood means that one is engaged in a trade or business, whose products or services are offered to the public at large. The offerings are made every business day — or virtually every business day — on a continuing basis. The offerings are made to customers and clients who pay a price, commission, or fee for the products or services accepted. These "gross receipts," as they are called, derive strictly from the acumen and skill of the entrepreneur: *not* from the mere passage of time. Certainly, in a trade or business, one must invest money in certain assets (buildings, equipment, inventory, labor, merchandise, etc.) in order to make a profit and derive income. The distinction key is **material participation** in one's trade or business.

It is true that an investor also invests money with the intention of making a profit. But it is doubtful that the profit motive in passive investments is essential to one's livelihood. In fact, an adage of investment wisdom states: "Do not invest money that you cannot afford to lose. And do not invest money for your sole source of livelihood. In a market crash, you could starve!"

The investment world and a trade or business are two different ballgames. Investors speak of "gross proceeds" whereas proprietors (entrepreneurs) refer to *gross receipts.* From their gross proceeds, investors determine their "gain or loss" of capital. In contrast, proprietors determine their "profit or loss" of income. An investor does not depend on the "bottom line" for his livelihood, whereas an entrepreneur does. We summarize in Figure 2.2 the distinctive attributes of investor versus entrepreneur.

Borderline Examples

The distinction between an investor and being in a trade or business is important not only for Social Security/Medicare tax purposes, but also for cost and expense accounting reasons. Let us illustrate the distinction with three examples: a stock broker, a land owner, and an antique clock collector.

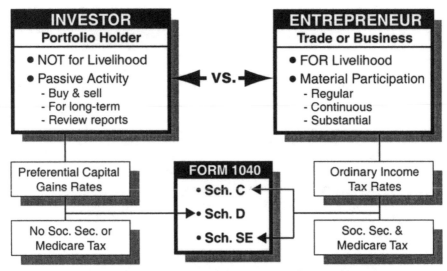

Fig. 2.2 - Tax Attributes: Investor vs. Entrepreneur

A stock broker is a person in the trade or business of buying and selling stocks, bonds, and securities for persons other than himself. He does this on a day-to-day basis for his clients. But he also may buy/sell some of the same stock and securities for his own account. In other words, he is both an investor and an entrepreneur (in a trade or business) at the same time. So, how does he distinguish his own investments from the trading of investments for his clients?

Answer: A special tax law applies. It is Section 1236(a) of the tax code. Its heading is: ***Dealers in Securities: Capital Gains***. Its principal wording reads as follows—

> *Gain by a dealer in securities from the sale or exchange of any security shall in no event be considered as gain from the sale or exchange of a capital asset unless—*
> *(1) the security was, before the close of the day on which it was acquired . . ., clearly identified in the dealer's records as a security held for investment; and*
> *(2) the security was not, at any time after the close of the day (or such earlier time), held by such dealer primarily for sale to customers in the ordinary course of his trade or business.*

So, a stock broker has to clearly identify his own investments and keep a separate, detailed record of them. Both of the Section 1236(a) requirements must be met. The second requirement mandates there be no commingling with customer transactions. Otherwise any gain on his own transactions is treated as ordinary income subject to the Social Security/Medicare tax.

In the case of a land owner, the distinction between holding land for investment purposes and for sale to customers in a trade or business is more difficult. Consider, for example, that a person bought a 50-acre tract of land. He decides to subdivide the tract into 1-acre parcels and sell them off a few at a time. Is he an investor, or is he a developer?

Another section of the tax code addresses this situation. This is Section 1237(a), headed as: ***Real Property Subdivided for Sale***. Pertinent excerpts read—

> *Any lot or parcel which is a part of a tract of real property in the hands of a taxpayer **other than a C corporation** shall not be deemed to be held primarily for sale to customers in the ordinary course of trade or business at the time of sale solely because of the taxpayer having subdivided such tract for purposes of sale or because of any activity incident to such subdivision or sale **if**—*
>
> *(1) such tract, or any lot or parcel thereof, had not been previously held by such taxpayer primarily for sale to customers . . .; **and***
>
> *(2) no substantial improvement that substantially enhances the value of the lot or parcel sold is made by the taxpayer . . .; **and***
>
> *(3) such lot or parcel, except in the case of real property acquired by inheritance or devise, is held by the taxpayer for a period of 5 years.* [Emphasis added.]

Section 1237 goes on to define the minimum number of parcel sales for capital gain purposes. It defines "necessary improvements" and "expenditures of sale." The subdivision of land for sale is a vast area of Tax Court litigation over capital gain versus ordinary gain. With the Social Security/Medicare tax rates so high these days, and with the taxable base — especially for Medicare —

(virtually) unlimited in amount, paying the "second tax" on real property investment gains is a horrifying example of how inattention to tax rules can get out of hand..

In the case of an antique clock collector, other special tax rules apply. Is the person an investor; is he a hobbyist; or is he a dealer? It all depends. He is taxed differently in each case.

Suppose the collector bought one or two antique clocks which were in need of repair. He had them professionally refurbished. Shortly thereafter, he offered them for sale at a profit. If this is all he did, he would be an investor. No Social Security/Medicare tax would apply.

Suppose he bought numerous old clocks, and did the repairs and renovations himself. He hung the clocks up in various rooms of his home. He showed them off frequently to his friends and guests. Occasionally, he would sell one or two to his friends, to get cash to buy other old clocks. He is a hobbyist. Section 183 would apply, namely: *Activities Not Engaged in for Profit*. His expenses would be allowable only to the extent of his sales receipts, each year. If a net gain, he would pay Social Security/Medicare tax. If a net loss, the loss would not be tax recognized.

If the collector bought and sold refurbished antique clocks frequently, advertised them regularly, and serviced the ones that he sold, he would be a dealer. Such activities are clearly a trade or business serving the general public. He would show an "operating" profit or loss at the end of each year. The profit is Social Security/Medicare taxed; the loss is tax recognized. The (entrepreneurial) loss can be used to offset other taxable sources of income, on page 1 of Form 1040.

Managing Own Investments?

Many taxpayers these days actively manage their own investments. They have a computer workstation at home; they subscribe to Internet, e-mail, and online services; and they maintain active financial accounts with one or more national and international brokerage houses. They buy software programs, advisory services, currency data, and investment reports from all over the world. They are online day in and day out switching their investments around, trying to maximize wealth . . . and trying to avoid losses. Are these persons investors, or are they traders?

This question has been ruled on in two particular cases: *F.R. Mayer* and *R.W. Steffler*. These two rulings are instructive in that they help you see the distinction through judicial eyes.

In *F.R. Mayer* [94-2 USTC ¶ 50,509; 32 Fed Cl 149], Mayer formed a corporation — The Captiva Corporation — of which he was the president and sole shareholder. He hired reputable money managers, bought computer networks, hired computer operating employees, paid rent, and incurred extensive commissions and expenses in connection with his $50,000,000 of investible assets. For the three years at tax issue, his "corporation" generated approximately $9,000,000 in long-term gains and approximately $6,000,000 in short-term gains. Some 1,338 separate capital transactions were involved. He claimed all of his investment activities as a business expense against the corporation, including his own $85,000 annual salary for each of the three years. The IRS disallowed all said expenses as being those of an investor, and not those of a trader. The Court concurred with the IRS.

The Court ruled that—

> The taxpayer's investment activities were not in the business of trading securities [for others] because . . . [his] orientation was toward long-term appreciation through capital investment rather than toward income from short-term trades made to take advantage of daily movement. Further, his involvement was non-active and indirect; he reviewed quarterly reports but did not personally make decisions regarding specific dates. . . . Therefore, expenses associated with the activity did not reduce the taxpayer's taxable income and did not reduce his alternative minimum taxable income.

In *R.W. Steffler* [T.C. Memo 1995–271; 69 TCM 2940, Dec. 50,703 (M)], Steffler and his wife (a math teacher and computer programmer) purchased 10 years of commodity market data, and formulated their own computer analysis for investment decisions. They purchased stationery, business cards, operating supplies, and commodity manuals, and opened a separate bank account in the name of "Steffler Enterprises." For the three years at tax issue, they purchased 78 commodities contracts for their own account. They devoted 20 to 40 hours per week of their time to commodity activities. They used their own money which, initially, was $100,000. They endured $31,560 in commodity losses. They wrote the losses off as a trade or business loss; not as a capital loss. The IRS said "No" and disallowed all losses and expenses therewith.

The Court sided with the IRS, by ruling that—

> The number of days [in a 3-year period] that the taxpayers purchased or sold contracts [78] leads us to conclude that they were investors in commodities and not traders. . . . [Furthermore], we conclude that the taxpayers have not shown that their commodities market activity was frequent, regular, and continuous enough to constitute trade or business.

Treatment of Investment Expenses

There is no question that if one has an extensive investment portfolio, and he keeps a persistent eye on his investments, he incurs various expenses. As we've seen above, they are not deductible as trade or business expenses. They are classed as *nonbusiness expenses* and are deductible — at least in part — under other tax law provisions.

Before any investment expenses can be deducted, they have to be categorized into three distinct groupings. The groupings are:

[1]   Expenses such as commissions, legal fees, etc., which have to be capitalized.

[2]   Expenses in the form of interest paid for borrowing investment money.

[3]   Expenses which are custodial, operational, and miscellaneous in type.

Commissions, legal fees, and transfer costs associated with the buying and selling of a capital asset are part of the cost of the asset itself. Such costs and expenses, therefore, are "capitalized." That is, they relate to the guarantee of ownership in the asset acquired or disposed. They are fully recoverable at time of sale . . . as one's "cost or other basis."

If you borrow money to carry on your investments, interest paid on that money is classed as *investment interest*. As per Section 163(d), investment interest paid is allowed as an itemized deduction on a special line on Schedule A (Form 1040). Before entry on Schedule A, however, Form 4952: *Investment Interest Expense Deduction*, must be completed.

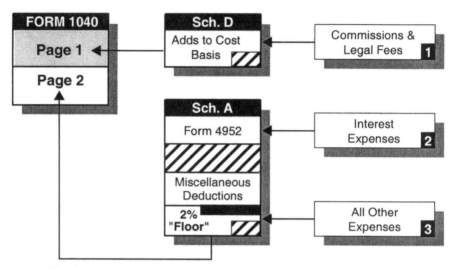

Fig. 2.3 - "Short Course" on Treatment of Investment Expenses

All other investment expenses — custodial fees, advisory reports, computer programs, utilities (phone, fax, online, e-mail, etc.), management fees, and so on — are classed simply as *miscellaneous expenses*. They, too, are allowable on Schedule A, but only if they exceed in amount what is termed: **the 2% AGI floor**. The rule on point is Section 67(a); its preamble reads—

In the case of an individual, the miscellaneous itemized deductions for any taxable year shall be allowed only to the extent that the aggregate of such deductions exceeds 2 percent of adjusted gross income [AGI].

For a depiction of the above treatment, we present Figure 2.3.

3

MATCHING PAYER REPORTINGS

> **TEFRA '82 Mandated A Whole New Tax Game In Capital Transactions. Starting Then, All Brokers, Middlemen, And Overseers Must Report To The IRS — On Forms 1099-B, Etc. — All Sales, Exchanges, And Other Dispositions Of Investment Assets. The GROSS PROCEEDS Must Be Reported For "Computer Matching": That IRS Dream Of Total Oversight Of All Investors. All Payer Reportings, Whether Correct Or Not, Are Treated As Being Gospel Truth. Thus, Achieving Matching Often Requires A "Straw Sale" (Or Two) For Adjustment Purposes. Recalcitrant Investors Are Subject To 28% Backup Withholding On Proceeds.**

We live in an electronic tax world. All brokers, financial institutions, barter exchangers, realty agents, and other intermediaries must report all capital transactions to the IRS. Each and every separate transaction — sale, exchange, rollover, redemption, or other transfer of a capital asset — must be reported. Annoying penalties are imposed on brokers for not doing so.

Those investors who live, dream, and conduct their capital transactions via online services in cyberspace — having a ball and thinking they are beyond the reach of the IRS — are in for a surprise. Interestingly, the IRS itself does not maintain any electronic surveillance over what you do; it puts pressure on your broker to track and report (at the end of each year) your investment activities. This is the modern day version of the 16th century practice of "tax farming."

Back in the 16th century, in monarchical Europe, revenue collections were made by "tax farming." Tax farmers were private entrepreneurs, commissioned by the reigning monarchs, to go out into the lands to force-collect revenue at whatever rates the traffic could bear. Out of this, there arose the practice of chain-whipping taxpayers to get them to report their sources of sustenance. Since then, tax revolutions have come and gone. But tax farming in the U.S. still persists. It is performed by private brokers reporting on their own customers and clients.

Chances are, you're at least partially familiar with the current broker reporting system. As an investor, surely you've already received one or more of those year-end *information returns*. We have a lot more to tell you about the system that you probably don't know. You won't find our information in those tax software programs you may buy, nor from your online service provider, nor from those fancy brochures your broker sends out. While you and your broker are busy making money, the IRS is busy perfecting ways to collect tax on that money.

Birth of TEFRA Concept

On August 13, 1981 the Economic Recovery Tax Act (ERTA) was enacted. Its central thrust was the reduction of the then maximum tax rate of 70% (for taxable incomes over $215,000 married) to 50% (for taxable incomes over $85,000 married). One does not have to be an economist to sense that this kind of rate and bracket reduction would cause severe revenue shortfalls. And, indeed it did. Individuals net earning over $85,000 made out like a bandit. Again, middle-income taxpayers bore the brunt . . . and raised hell with Congress.

Defensive about "favoring the rich," Congress looked to the IRS for ideas on how to raise revenues without raising tax rates above 50%. With its experience and success with employer Form W-2 mandates (Wage and Tax Statements), it proposed a similar mandate on *all payers* of money (and property) to taxpayers. Thrilled by the idea, Congress and the President, on September 3, 1982, enacted the *Tax Equity and Fiscal Responsibility Act*: TEFRA. This Act was heralded as a "revenue enhancement" (the *tax equity* part) and "tax punishment" (the *fiscal responsibility* part) measure. The real target of TEFRA was the imposition of mandatory reportings by other than employers, and the pyramiding of penalties for revenue enhancement.

Among TEFRA's 200 added provisions of tax law, vigorous new reporting rules were enacted. Most pertinent to our coverage in this book is the TEFRA section on "Broker Transactions Reports." The Act defines in broad terms who a broker is, for information reporting purposes. It gives the IRS additional powers to require reporting the *gross proceeds* on every sale or exchange executed for a customer. Of particular interest to us are the two TEFRA definitions of a broker and a customer.

TEFRA defines a "broker" as—

Any person who (for a consideration) regularly acts as a middleman with respect to property or services.

This encompasses anyone and everyone in the business world who performs a brokerage-type service for a commission or fee. This includes stock brokers, bond dealers, neighborhood bankers, savings institutions, real estate agents, mortgage lenders, title companies, account executives, financial advisers, mutual fund managers, insurance adjusters, coin exchangers, barter arrangers, commodity traders, futures contractors, and the like. This broker definition is all-sweeping.

TEFRA defines a "customer" as—

Any person for whom a broker has transacted any business.

The term "any business" means a brokerage transaction involving: (a) transfer of property, (b) redemption of securities, (c) retirement of indebtedness, or (d) closing a transaction (in commodities, personal property, or real property). So if one pays a commission or fee for selling, exchanging, or otherwise transferring any capital asset, he/she is a "customer" of a broker.

TEFRA goes on to require that every customer must supply to a broker his/her own Social Security number. The number must be provided every time a capital transaction is executed by a different broker. If there were 20 different-broker transactions in a given year, for example, the customer would have to furnish his/her

Social Security number 20 times for that year. A customer who fails to do so is subject to a $50 penalty . . . for each failure.

Brokers, too, are subject to the TEFRA penalty. If a broker fails to file an information return with the IRS for each transaction that he executes for a customer, he can be penalized $50 for each such failure. Furthermore, he can be penalized up to $100,000 for cumulative failures in any calendar year. If he intentionally disregards the reporting rules of TEFRA, he can be penalized 5% of the gross proceeds that he transacts, without limit. This could pretty well wipe out his entire brokerage commissions every year.

Code Section 6045

The statutory force for reporting all capital transactions is embodied in Section 6045 of the Internal Revenue Code. This section is captioned: *Returns of Brokers*.

This is a good example of misleading captions in tax law. Section 6045 does not pertain to the personal income tax returns of brokers themselves. Instead, it prescribes *information returns* to be submitted by brokers. Thus, a more appropriate caption would have been: Information Returns **by** Brokers (not "of").

Section 6045(a): *General Rule*, prescribes the general reporting mandate. It is sufficiently important to our discussion that we quote it in full. It reads—

Every person doing business as a broker shall, when required by the [IRS], make a return, in accordance with such regulations as the [IRS] may prescribe, showing the name and address of each customer, with such details regarding gross proceeds and such other information as the [IRS] may by forms or regulations require with respect to such business.

Initially, the IRS-prepared regulations under Section 6045 amounted to about 5,000 words. Currently, the count is over 35,000 words! They start with Regulation 1.6045-1 titled: *Returns of information of broker and barter exchanges*, and extend through 1.6045-5: *Information reporting on payments to attorneys.* Obviously, these regulations on mandatory reportings are much too extensive for a complete discussion here.

Despite the extensiveness of Regulation 1.6045-1, at least one selected excerpt is instructive. Consider the term "gross proceeds," for example. Regulation 1.6045-1(d)(5) specifically says—

The gross proceeds on a sale are the total amount paid to the customer or credited to the customer's account as a result of such sale.

Now, for the practical effect. Suppose a customer buys a 5-year Treasury Bond for $10,000. After a year or so, he sells the bond through a broker for $9,765. He has a capital *loss* of $235. Is there any federal tax revenue to be gained on the $235 loss? Of course not. Then, why does the broker have to report the $9,765 gross proceeds?

It is not just the $50 penalty revenue that your government wants. There is a more insidious reason. It is called "backup withholding." It is that Form W-2 mindset that the IRS has.

Backup Withholding: 28%

TEFRA introduced a whole new concept in federal tax administration. It set forth a punitive procedure called *backup withholding*. Today, a backup withholding amount equal to 28% of gross proceeds can be imposed. This is for not reporting on one's return his gross sale proceeds, even when a capital loss is sustained. The emphasis is not on the correct amount of your gain or loss, but on your correct gross proceeds.

Punitive power was granted to the IRS by a whole new section of the tax code, namely, Section 3406: ***Backup Withholding***. The essence of relevance here is—

In the case of any reportable payment . . . (relating to returns of brokers) . . . if the payee fails to furnish his [Social Security number], *or . . .* [underreports his transactions] *. . . the payer shall deduct and withhold from such payment a tax equal to 28 percent of such payment.*

It is important that you be aware that, **in addition** to ordinary withholdings on your salaries and wages, a 28% withholding on your capital transactions can be imposed. It *will be* imposed if you fail to report on your tax return three or more transactions in a single year. Three or more failures are IRS-treated as intentional disregard and willful neglect.

Let's go back to the example of our Treasury Bond sale above. Suppose a customer made three T-bond sales in a taxable year. One sale was $9,675 (a $235 *loss*); another was $9,885 (a $115 *loss*); and the third was $10,350 (a $350 gain). His cumulative loss and gain for the three sales would be exactly zero, that is: 350 gain – 235 – 115 = 0. There would be no net tax consequence whatsoever. Realizing this, as an investor, you decide not to report the three sales. "After all," you say to yourself, "I owe no tax on these transactions."

Three failures to report a capital transaction on one's Form 1040 will be noted by the IRS's Big Computer. Thereupon, the IRS can direct the broker to withhold 28% of your gross proceeds. In the example case, the gross proceeds would be $30,000. Therefore, 28% of the $30,000 — which is $8,400 — would be withheld by the broker and paid over to the IRS. The amount withheld, however, is treated as prepayment credit against your final taxes for that year. What does this do for government?

If there were no additional tax due — as could well be the case in the example presented — the entire $8,400 backup withholding would be refunded to you. It would take 12 to 18 months after the withholding, before the refund would be paid. In the meantime, the government has held your $8,400 *interest free*. At, say, 6% per annum ordinary interest, the government would derive $756 in undeserved revenue. This is called the "withholding float" principle of TEFRA compliance.

Taxing Gross Proceeds

There is still another insidious purpose of broker reportings. The purpose is to tax the *gross proceeds* of those who underreport, or who do not report, or who do not report correctly. With the IRS's mindset, it is so easy to tax gross proceeds. *It is wrong . . .* but it is computer-easy, and difficult for a taxpayer to correct.

Most taxpayers are terrified of the IRS. They are easily intimidated by its computer printouts. The printouts are unintelligible, and are designed to shock taxpayers into prompt payment of additional tax, penalties, and interest without questioning the legitimacy of the computer demand. You have to suppress your anger, and find the fine print that says: *If you do not agree with our statement* (etc.).

To illustrate the effect, let's go back to the three T-bond sales above. The net gain and loss for tax purposes is zero. But, by not reporting the three sales, the computer will tax the $30,000 gross proceeds as though it were additional ordinary income. Suppose the taxpayer were in the 15% tax bracket (single), without the sales. With the sales, suppose the tax bracket jumped to 30% (single). Thus, the computer would demand $9,000 in *additional tax*. To this would be added the Section 6662 accuracy-related *penalty* of 20% (another $1,800). Since it would take from 18 to 24 months for the IRS to notify the taxpayer, there would be approximately $1,600 of *interest* to be paid. Altogether, a computer demand for $12,400.

You don't think this could happen?

It *did* happen!

It happened to an 86-year-old woman (widow), who was disabled and bedridden. When her daughter told her about the additional tax, she had a stroke. When she recovered, she told her daughter to draw down her life's savings and pay the computer demand in full without questioning it.

Fortunately, the daughter went to a professional tax person to review the situation. The IRS was dead wrong. While the elderly woman did not report the T-bond sales on her Form 1040, she did report all of the interest income from the T-bonds. Some common sense could have been used by the IRS. Eventually, the matter was straightened out, and there was no additional tax to pay.

Broker/Payer Reportings

How is a broker to report and withhold on the gross proceeds of a capital transaction? Answer: With a W-2-like form.

The means for broker reporting is addressed by Regulation 1.6045-1(d)(2). Subheaded as *Transactional reporting*, it reads:

> *As to each sale with respect to which a broker is required to make a return of information under this section, the broker . . .*

shall show on Form 1099 the name, address, and taxpayer identification of the customer for whom the sale was effected, the property sold, . . . **the gross proceeds, sale date,** *and such other information as may be required on Form 1099, in the form, manner, and number of copies required by Form 1099-B. . . .* **A copy of Form 1099** *. . . shall be furnished to the customer on or before January 31 of the year following the year for which the return . . . was required to be made.*

Editorial Note: The reference to "Form 1099" is to a series of 16 Forms 1099. The three most significant for Schedule D purposes are: 1099-B, 1099-DIV, and 1099-S.

Form 1099-B carries the official heading: ***Proceeds from Broker and Barter Exchange Transactions***. An edited version of the official form is presented in Figure 3.1.

PAYER'S name, address & zip code		**YEAR**		**PROCEEDS FROM BROKER AND BARTER**
		1a. Date of Sale		
		1b. CUSIP No.		
PAYER'S Tax I.D.No.	RECIPIENT'S Soc.Sec.No.	2. Stocks, bonds, etc.		☐ Gross Proceeds ☐ Net Proceeds
RECIPIENT'S name, address & zip code		3. Bartering		4. Fed. tax withheld
		5.	6.	Corp. restructuring exchanges
		Regulated Futures Contracts		
		7.	8.	9.	10.	11.	12.
Copy A	Copy B	Copy C	*Edited for instructional purposes*	

Fig. 3.1 - General Format/Content of Form 1099-B for Broker/Payers

Please study Figure 3.1 carefully. If you are an investor, and make any sales or exchanges or other transfers of a capital asset through a broker, *each transaction* will be reported to the IRS on this format (or on subsequent amendments to it). Note that Box 1a requires the date of sale. Box 1b requires reporting the CUSIP Number (Committee on Uniform Security Identification

Procedures). The ultimate IRS goal is to have all capital transactions taking place in the U.S. be traceable through their gross proceeds and brokerage account numbers.

In Figure 3.1 particularly note Box 2: Stocks, bonds, etc. The "etc." means *all* capital transactions (commodities, currencies, collectibles) except bartering (Box 3), corporate restructuring (Boxes 5 and 6), and futures contracts (Boxes 7 through 12).

In the same space as Box 2, there are two checkboxes:

☐ *Gross proceeds*

☐ *Net proceeds*

The net proceeds are gross proceeds less broker commissions, closing costs, and option premiums. More frequently than not, these two checkboxes are left blank. If so, assume that gross proceeds are reported.

At present, three copies of each Form 1099-B are required. Copy A goes to the Internal Revenue Service, Copy B goes to the recipient (investor/payee), and Copy C is retained by the preparing broker (payer) for his files. In practice, Copy B is the only physical piece of paper involved. "Copies" A and C are purely electronic media transmissions.

A carefully worded preprinted instruction on Copy B: *For Recipient*, reads:

> *This is important tax information and is being furnished to the* [IRS]. *If you are required to file a return, a negligence penalty or other sanction* [backup withholding] *may be imposed on you if this income is taxable and the IRS determines that it has not been reported.*

This instruction by the IRS, and a similar substitute instruction by your broker, put you on "Official Notice." This is your warning that you are subject to backup withholding and to full taxation on your gross proceeds, if you fail to report and match that which your broker reports, or that which other payers report. The problem is: There are so many different-purpose 1099s — 16 by recent count, each with a different official or substitute format — that conscientious recipients are truly confused.

Search for "Substitute Statements"

Very few brokerage firms, banks, insurance companies, mutual funds, or other financial institutions actually furnish you a piece of paper formatted similar to that in Figure 3.1. It is just too much of a hassle to spoon feed each customer with all the transactional information he needs to prepare his own tax return. It is therefore not surprising that many brokerage firms have objected to the increased administrative cost imposed on them by the requirements of Form 1099-B (and other 1099s).

As a consequence of these objections, the IRS allows brokers to provide their clients with *equivalent substitute statements*. Generally, this equivalence is construed to mean a broker's regular (buy, sell, exchange, etc.) confirmation statements, modified as necessary to accommodate the 1099-B and other 1099 reporting procedures. More often than not, the "modifications" are confusing and misleading, and difficult to identify.

Some brokerage firms computer-print the phrase "Form 1099" onto their regular year-end cumulative statements. Thereon is a preprinted headnote or footnote that reads:

When this statement is marked 1099, the information above will be filed with the IRS pursuant to federal law.

Other brokerage firms will prepare a consolidated year-end statement of all transactions for each client. In their own computer format, they will separate out the various 1099 reportings. They will indicate specific dollar entries, blanks, or footnotes on sequential lines marked, such as:

	Amount	Description
• **Form 1099-B**	_____	_____
• Form 1099-C	_____	_____
• Form 1099-INT	_____	_____
• **Form 1099-DIV**	_____	_____
• Form 1099-OID	_____	_____
• Form 1099-MISC	_____	_____
• Form 1099-R	_____	_____
• **Form 1099-S**	_____	_____

Thus, instead of issuing separate 1099 forms, one computer form with separated amounts is issued. This is an equivalent substitute statement for IRS reporting purposes.

There is no uniformity in format or placement of the reported information on these substitute statements. Each broker does that which is most compatible with his own internal computer programming and confirmation procedures. Many brokers "pump out" their 1099 confirmation statements as though in a year-end tidal wave. Some send duplicates; some send corrections; some refuse to make corrections.

As an investor, you must search diligently through all substitute statements. You want particularly to separate out those marked "1099" in some manner. You must *read* all of the computer forms to do this. The IRS will not do it for you.

We cannot caution you too strongly to be on the alert for spotting that broker information which is SUBSTITUTE reported to the IRS. If you are not keenly selective in this regard, the IRS will computer demand from you additional tax.

How "Computer Matching" Works

On an average *slow* stock-trading day in the U.S., some 800,000,000 (800 million) shares change hands on the New York and American exchanges. Another 200,000,000 (200 million) shares, contracts, and equivalents change hands over the counter and through regional exchanges and mark-to-market sales. Assuming an average of 100 shares per transaction, there could be as many as 3,000,000,000 (3 billion) Form 1099-Bs filed with the IRS each year (in 250 trading days). Can you not imagine the confusion and chaos that result?

Think of the inadvertent errors that are made. The broker makes errors. The broker's computer makes errors. The IRS key punch operators make errors. The overall result is a barrage of computer mismatching problems that boggles the human mind.

The idea behind all of these 1099 forms is for the IRS's computer to cross-match the information on the 1099s with the information reported on each individual's own 1040 tax return with Schedule D attached. This is the "compliance enforcement" aspects of the 1099s. If there is a mismatch, the computer automatically assesses an additional tax . . . plus penalty and interest. The grand scheme is presented in Figure 3.2. It is the perfect dream for IRS oversight of **all** investors .

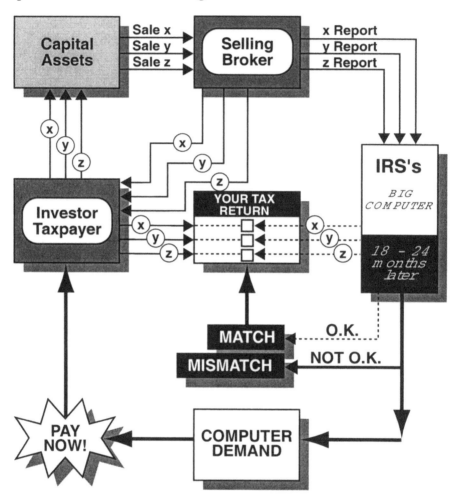

Fig. 3.2 - Scheme of IRS's "Computer Matching" of Gross Proceeds

Let us now exemplify the problem. Consider an investor who has made five capital transactions for the year (3 short-term and 2 long-term). His total proceeds from the five sales are $100,000. He made $15,000 profit on the three short sales; he suffered a $10,000 loss on the two long sales. For his own convenience, he groups the three short sales into one entry on Form 1040. He lists the average sales price of $25,000. He also groups the two long sales into one entry, and lists the average sales price of $5,000. Total sales reported: $30,000. His gain and loss entries are absolutely correct. He computes and pays the correct tax. What happens in the computer matching process? (Assume the taxpayer is in the 30% bracket.)

Some 18 to 24 months later, the IRS computer picks up the fact that five Form 1099-Bs were submitted showing total proceeds of $100,000. It matches this information with the $30,000 total sales shown on the individual's Form 1040. It computes a reporting discrepancy of $70,000. The computer immediately asserts a deficiency demand for $21,000 in additional tax ($70,000 x 30%) plus, say $3,000 in interest. No IRS human ever reads the proper gain and loss information on Schedule D (Form 1040). The computer does everything. When the taxpayer gets the Computer Demand, does he owe the additional tax and interest?

No. He does not.

He reported his proper gain and loss, and he paid the correct tax thereon. For his own convenience, he simply lumped his five transactions into two, and reported the average gross sales proceeds of each. What is so wrong with this? After all, the correct *taxable* amount was reported.

Which brings up the disturbing question. What is the real purpose of Form 1099-B? It does not — cannot — establish the correct tax. Nor does it verify actual reporting compliance.

Misperception by the IRS

Glance again at Figure 3.1 showing the required entries on Form 1099-B. Then, from your own records, select a Form W-2 Wage and Tax Statement. Note the general similarity in format between your W-2 and the 1099-B.

A broker who pays the proceeds in a capital transaction is regarded by the IRS much the same as an employer who pays wages and other compensation for personal services. This is a basic failing in perception by the IRS.

Capital transactions and wage income are tax treated much differently from each other. We particularly stressed this difference in Chapter 2: How "Investor" Tax Defined. The IRS knows about this difference, but it looks the other way in its mandate for computer compliance by taxpayers.

In capital transactions, tax applies only after netting of gains and losses, both short-term and long-term. In contrast, tax applies to wage income directly. Yet, in the IRS computer center, the 1099-B gross proceeds are treated computationally exactly the same as W-2 gross wages.

To illustrate the incompatibility in tax treatment, let's go back to our five-transaction example above. For illustrative simplicity, assume that the taxpayer is in a constant 30% tax bracket. Recall that the broker-reported gross proceeds were $100,000. The broker properly submitted to the IRS five Forms 1099-B.

The correct taxable amount reported by the taxpayer on his Form 1040 was $5,000. This is the result of net-netting $15,000 of gain with $10,000 of loss. For the assumptions made, the correct tax on the $5,000 would be $1,500 (30% x $5,000).

If the $100,000 were all wages, as the IRS assumes, the computer tax would be $30,000!

Now do you see the basic injustice and fallibility of the computer compliance effort with Form 1099-B?

Turning the matter around, suppose the taxpayer matched exactly on his Form 1040 the gross proceeds reported on Forms 1099-B. In his preoccupation with exact matching, he erroneously reported the $15,000 capital gain as a $15,000 loss. The result would be an underpayment of tax by $900. (The per year capital loss limit is $3,000. So, 30% x $3,000 equals $900.)

Will the IRS computer pick up this erroneous underpayment?

No. It will not.

Our overall conclusion is that Form 1099-B serves no correct tax purpose whatsoever, where the taxpayer, broker, and IRS computer exactly match each other. Otherwise, its only purpose is an "irritant and prod" to those taxpayer/investors who are habitually indifferent to their tax reporting duties. We know of actual cases where the IRS has erroneously computer billed nonmatching investors, who have simply paid the bill without contesting it. If you have good reason for believing that the IRS's mismatching notice is wrong, you have a duty to advise the IRS of the error(s).

Role of "Straw Sales"

At this point, now, we can let you in on a little-known secret. Knowing it and using it, will help avert those irritating proddings — computer mismatching notices and demands — from the IRS. Always report on your tax return a total gross sales figure that *equals or exceeds* the total amount electronically reported to the IRS by your broker(s). For example, if your broker reports $31,540 and you report $32,450, that's O.K. The IRS always accepts the highest total proceeds amount, whether by you, your broker, or some combination thereof.

How do you accomplish the exact matching or greater-than-matching reportings?

Answer: Use one or more "straw sales," as necessary. A straw sale is an *accounting adjustment* only. It is an adjustment entry in the "sales price" column of Schedule D. Enter whatever amount you need to establish the computer match that the IRS wants to see. Then immediately offset the straw amount with an equal amount of cost. This way, there are no additional gain or loss amounts to move through your other gain/loss computations on Schedule D.

For example, suppose that on one of your broker Forms 1099-B, there is a $10,000 "correctional transaction." That is, you directed the sum of $10,000 into a growth-income account, but your broker assigned it to your equity-income account by mistake. When the matter is called to his attention, the broker withdraws the $10,000 and reassigns it to the correct account. At the end of the year, the IRS requires that your broker report the $10,000 as a transactional proceeds amount. This is what we call an *accounting discrepancy* which is a quite common occurrence.

Do not argue with your broker on this matter. He has "federal law" to follow; he also has his own internal accounting procedures to follow. You take the initiative and do the adjustment on your return. But do not distort your true net gain or loss in any way.

Enter the $10,000 as the sales price, and immediately offset it with a $10,000 cost item. The transactional gain is "zero"; the transactional loss is also zero. You have made a straw adjustment in such a way that you satisfy the IRS's matching computer without altering your tax consequences.

If you have more than one broker reporting to the IRS, enter an adjusting straw sale (as necessary) for each broker separately. You want to be able to pinpoint which broker, or which transactional event, is a source of error or miscommunication. The general scheme involved is presented in Figure 3.3. By entering zero (-0-) in the gain/loss column on Schedule D, you are disclosing to the IRS that you are making a matching adjustment only . . . without skewing your tax results.

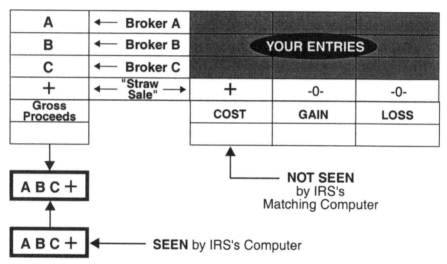

Fig. 3.3 - What the IRS's Computer "Sees". . . and Does Not "See"

Nominee Reportings

It is bad enough having a broker or other payer middleperson reporting your investment transactions to the IRS. Worse yet, there are situations where *you* — the reported-on person — have to report on other persons: your own family and friends. These situations are called *nominee* transactions.

A "nominee" is a person who is one of the designated recipients of the sales proceeds from a co-ownership transaction. If, for example, there are three co-owners who have pooled their money, one of the co-owners may take it upon himself/herself to be the nominee for the others. If no such voluntary designation is made, the reporting broker uses the name he knows, or selects the first name in alphabetical order. The "nominee" thereby becomes the person whose name and Social Security number are reported to the IRS as receiving the entire sales proceeds.

To illustrate what we are getting at, let's take a common example of nominee activities.

You are a reasonably astute investor held in much regard by your family, friends, and colleagues. Two of your friends get a hot investment tip. They approach you to pool their money with you to have you buy — through your broker — 500 shares of a new public offering of XYZ Biotech. Each of the three of you puts up $2,000 (total: $6,000). Sure enough, within 30 days, the XYZ stock triples in value. You instruct your broker to sell. After deducting his commission, he sends you a check for $17,628.

Whose name and Social Security number are going on the Form 1099-B (or any other 1099 form) when the broker reports the $17,628 sales proceeds to the IRS?

Answer: Your name, of course.

And who is going to pay tax on the $17,628?

You are . . . UNLESS.

Your alternative is to re-report one-third of the sale proceeds ($5,876) under the name and Social Security number of Friend A. You do likewise for Friend B. You do this as a **nominee filer**. That is, you prepare **Form 1096**: *Annual Summary and Transmittal of U.S. Information Returns*, and attach to it a Form 1099-B for Friend A, and a Form 1099-B for Friend B (total of two attachments). You send the transmittal form with the two 1099s attached to the IRS. Mailing instructions on "Where to File" are on the back of Form 1096. You send each friend a copy of his 1099 for preparing his own Schedule D.

If you do not make the two re-reports as nominee, you wind up paying capital gains tax on $15,628 (17,628 – 2,000). By separately reporting each of your friends' share to the IRS, you pay tax only on $3,876 (5,876 – 2,000).

A simpler way than the 1096/1099 re-reportings is to use the straw sale technique in Figure 3.3. That is, you report on Schedule D of your return the total gross proceeds ($17,628) less your cost

($2,000) for a *tentative* net gain of $15,628. Then immediately below this entry, you show the two nominee sales as follows:

Description	Gross Proceeds	Cost	Gain/<Loss>
XYZ Biotech	17,628	2,000	15,628
Nominee A			
- name & SSN	-0-	5,876	<5,876>
Nominee B			
- name & SSN	-0-	5,876	<u><5,876></u>
		Net Gain	3,876

The $3,876 amount is the same true net gain as above.

You've got to do *something*! Do it the technically correct way (by formal re-reportings) or the simpler way (on Schedule D). Otherwise, you are the nominee fall guy.

You have to admit it. The IRS has come up with a masterful scheme of tax farming.

4

COST OR OTHER BASIS

When Selling A Capital Asset, Your Primary Concern [For Schedule D, Column (e) Purposes] Is Full Recovery Of Your Invested Money. When Shares Or Units Are Purchased, Costing Methods Include: (A) Specific Designation, (B) First-In, First-Out, (C) Cost Averaging, And (D) Cumulative Costing. The Cost Basis Of Mutual Fund Shares With Multiple Dividend Rollovers Can Be Confusing. "Other Basis" Rules Apply To Acquisitions By Exchange, Gift, Inheritance, And Substitution. Where Basis Records Are Tangled, Jumbled, Or Poorly Kept, Use The "Best Evidence" That You Can Find. Otherwise, ZERO BASIS Is Presumed.

Capital gain or loss occurs to an investor only when he sells an asset: not when he buys it. Until a sale or exchange — or other disposition — takes place, there is no way to fix the amount of gain or loss. Furthermore, it is the character of the asset at time of sale that determines whether it is a capital asset. The character may change between time of acquisition and time of disposition. Also, its cost or other basis may change. Whatever the change, the dominant concern is to recover all of one's capital investment. Doing so means that said amount is not taxed. It represents neither gain nor loss.

The term "cost" means the purchase price of property when (in the form of a capital asset) it is sold. The term "other basis" means the cost equivalent when an asset is acquired by other than purchase. The term "sold" means sale, exchange, or other disposition. These terms, simple as they may sound, are extremely important to an investor. Ignoring the importance of simple terms can mean higher tax burdens than necessary.

For example, almost every investor knows what a "sale or exchange" is. But how many know what an "other disposition" is?

Not all transfers of property are effected by sale or exchange. There are many situations where property is conveyed for other than full and adequate consideration. Examples are gift, inheritance, theft, casualty, bankruptcy, abandonment, worthlessness, termination of a trust, dissolution of a partnership, liquidation of a corporation, involuntary conversion, government mandates, court-ordered transfers, and so on. All of these dispositions are treated as sales (or exchanges) for capital accounting purposes. If you ignore these dispositions, as many investors tend to do, you do so at your own tax peril. Since the IRS knows your gross sale proceeds (à la Chapter 3), it will tax these gross proceeds as ordinary income unless you set forth your "cost or other basis" properly on Schedule D (1040).

In this chapter, therefore, we want to explain more fully those factors that establish your cost or other basis when an asset is sold. Establishing said basis for tax purposes is not as simple as you may off-hand think. It requires a lot of homework and recordkeeping which distracts from the "fun and games" of active investing. However, if you intensely dislike keeping adequate cost basis records, there is one simple, safe solution. You can always assume zero basis, and pay tax on the full gross proceeds! But why do this? Why not make a good faith *estimate* and see what happens?

Column (e): The Focus

In the preceding chapter, we stressed the importance of computer matching the sales price as it appears in column (d) on Schedule D (1040). Now we want to focus exclusively on column (e). Said column is captioned:

Cost or other basis. See instructions.

The term "See instructions" refers to an 8-page 3-columnar text of about 15,000 words. The text is titled:

Instructions for Schedule D, Capital Gains and Losses

These instructions address personal use of capital assets, nondeductible losses, and items for special treatment.

As an example of the kind of wording found in the official instructions, we cite the opening paragraph in the section headed: *Column (e) — Cost or Other Basis*. It reads—

In general, the cost or other basis is the cost of the property plus purchase commissions and improvements, minus depreciation, amortization, and depletion. If you inherited the property, got it as a gift, or received it in a tax-free exchange, involuntary conversion, or a "wash sale" of stock, you may not be able to use the actual cost as the basis. If you do not use the actual cost, attach an explanation of your basis.

Then, some six paragraphs later, you are instructed:

For more details, see Publication 551. [Basis of Assets]

The introduction to Publication 551 reads in pertinent part—

Basis is the amount of your investment in property for tax purposes. Use the basis . . . to figure gain or loss on the sale or other disposition of property. You must keep accurate records of all items that affect the basis of property so you can make these computations. . . . Your original basis in property is adjusted (increased or decreased) by certain events. If you make improvements to the property, increase your basis. If you take deductions for depreciation or casualty losses, reduce your basis [when the property is sold].

These and related official instructions, forms, and publications are telling you that establishing your tax basis is not a one-time static event. It is a "moving target," so to speak. You have to track the target strictly on your own. You put money in, you take money out. Because so, your basis may vary between, or be a combination of, four distinct versions. The four versions are:

(a) *Cost basis* — actual traceable money (or money's worth in property) put into or taken out of the asset acquired.

(b) *Other basis* — equivalent market value or basis transfer when an asset is acquired other than through direct purchase or exchange.

(c) *Adjusted basis* — when improvements or additions are made (to the already acquired asset), or when allowable deductions are tax claimed.

(d) *Allocated basis* — splitting or cloning an asset between its acquisition and disposition, and proportionalizing its basis (for each portion "partitioned").

All of these basis variants are unbrellaed under the collective tax term: *Cost or other basis.* For example, the instructions say—

If you sold stock, adjust your basis by subtracting all the nontaxable distributions you received before the sale. Also, adjust your basis for any stock splits.

As indicated previously, the collective basis term is column (e) on Schedule D (1040). In the most self-interest sense possible, column (e) is the PIVOTAL ROLE between the sale price amount and the gain or loss amount for taxation purposes. We depict this role for you in Figure 4.1. Column (e) represents **your** *return of capital.* As such, it is not taxed! Therefore, it should be in your self-interest to make all column (e) entries as painstakingly complete as possible. Our Figure 4.1 should convince you that neither your broker, nor the IRS, really cares what you enter in column (e). That is, so long as you can support each entry amount with convincing backup records.

Must "Capitalize" Costs, Etc.

A capital transaction consists of three distinct phases. There is acquisition of the asset (Phase I); there is the holding of that asset over some period of time (Phase II); and there is disposition of it (Phase III). There is no capital accounting until the asset is relinquished to someone else by sale, exchange, or other disposition.

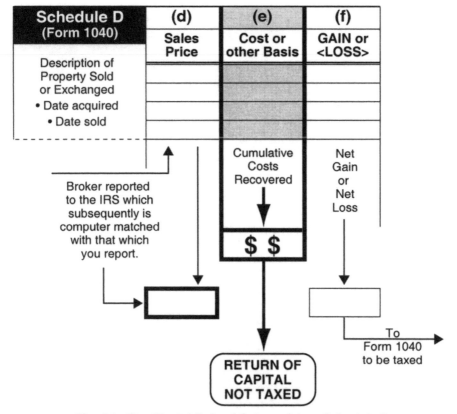

Fig. 4.1 - The Pivotal Role of Column (e) on Schedule D

Because there is no capital accounting until sale of an asset, investors tend to get careless in their recordkeeping duties. The longer the span of time between acquisition and disposition, the more inattentive and lethargic they become. The greater the number of transactions in a taxable year, the more troublesome and confusing the records become.

It is nice to make money on one's investments, and it is painful to lose it. It is even more painful (to some taxpayers) to keep proper records on each investment. Nevertheless, it is your duty to do so. The position of the IRS is this: If you do not keep complete records on *each transaction*, your gross proceeds (at time of sale) are treated as **all gain**! You are maximum taxed accordingly.

All of which brings us to a very important tax accounting point. All costs, carrying charges, and basis adjustments associated with an investment asset must be *capitalized*. That is, you must keep a running record of your costs, charges, and adjustments as you go along. When these items are capitalized, they define the tax basis of the asset. They are accumulated, then *subtracted* from the gross proceeds received at time of disposition. An illustration of what we are getting at here is presented in Figure 4.2.

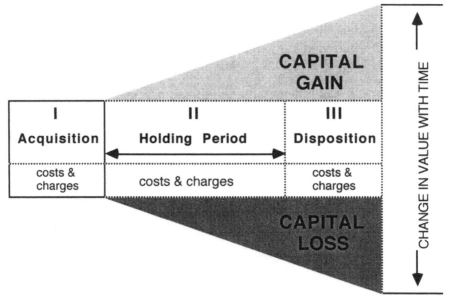

Fig.4.2 - Capitalization of Costs until Asset Disposition

Note in Figure 4.2 that we use the term "cost and charges" at each of the three different asset phases. At time of acquisition, in addition to your purchase cost (or other basis, if not purchased), there are add-on costs and charges such as sales tax, transfer taxes, title costs, legal costs (when clear title is in dispute), appraisal fees, loan fees (if money is borrowed to acquire the asset), recording fees, handling and shipping, and the like.

While holding an asset, there are also costs, charges, and adjustments. There could be storage, security, and verification charges, for example. There could be additions to (such as dividend rollovers) or subtractions from (such as nontaxable distributions) the asset while being held. If it is a tangible asset, there could be improvements to it or deductions from it in the form of depreciation allowances, insurance reimbursement, or "partial sales" (for which money has been received). To account for these receipts, your basis has to be reduced.

When an asset is relinquished to a new owner, there are advertising costs, sales commissions, closing expenses, transfer taxes, warranty costs, recording fees, and the like. Whatever cost, expense, charge, or guarantee is directly associated with the asset being held and sold, is a capitalized cost.

There is, we think, one clear message in our Figure 4.2. All of that white space you see marked as "costs & charges" represents your cumulative tax basis in that asset which you are readying for sale. It should be self-evident, therefore, that no one but you is going to track and record such vital tax information. All that "white space" represents your money being held by others, until the asset is sold. The idea is to get all your basis money back, tax free. You've previously paid tax on it.

There is also a subliminal message in Figure 4.2. If there is no change in market value between time of acquisition and time of sale, there is no tax to pay. You've obviously made neither gain nor loss. This occurs when the sales proceeds exactly equal your cost or other basis in that asset. You signify this to the IRS by entering zero (- 0 -) in the gain or loss column on Schedule D.

Cost Basis in Stock Shares

The most common example of cost basis concerns is the buying and selling of stock shares in Corporate America (or Corporate World). Each share of stock purchased represents a fractional ownership interest in a publicly tradeable capital asset. Usually the shares are purchased a batch at a time. A "batch" may be 10 shares, 100 shares, 1,000 shares, or more. The shares may be purchased in a designated corporate entity (through a stock broker) or a designated mutual fund (through a fund manager).

Unless an investor is a "day trader" (like a stock broker or fund manager), one tends to purchase his shares (in a favored entity) over a period of time. The acquisition time period may span one year, three years, ten years, or more. The longer the acquisition time, the more difficult it is to keep adequate cost basis records. When the time comes to sell, the tax accounting problem is always the same. What is the cost basis of each share sold?

Let us illustrate the concern in the most simple terms possible. You are fascinated by the growth potential of the XYZ corporation (or mutual fund). Over a period of several years, you buy the following number of shares at the following prices:

Purchase	No. of Shares	$ per Share	$ Cost
No. 1	50 sh	8.00/sh	400
No. 2	75 sh	9.60/sh	720
No. 3	150 sh	10.50/sh	1,575
No. 4	100 sh	9.40/sh	940
Totals	375 sh		3,635

To simplify the cost basis question further, let us assume, for the moment, that there are no dividend distributions, no stock splits, no stock bonuses, and no returns of capital while the above 375 shares are being held. We'll come back to these "distribution matters" later.

The XYZ share price goes to $12.50 per share. You decide to sell 100 shares. Which 100 shares do you sell, and what is your cost basis in the 100 shares sold?

Before answering, retrieve from your records each of the four purchase confirmation statements prepared by your broker. Mark them sequentially as #1, #2, etc. You'll need to make further markings on these statements for the shares sold.

For cost basising, there are three ways that you can go. There is: (a) the specific identification method, (b) the first-in, first-out method, and (c) the average cost method. For each batch sold, you must stick to one method only. If you sell three separate batches, you can use method (a) for batch 1, method (b) for batch 2, and method (c) for batch 3. Using the data above, let us illustrate each of these methods separately.

The "Specific Identification" Method

The specific identification (SID) method of cost basising requires that you identify to your broker (or fund manager) which of your purchased shares you want sold. You make this identification by purchase date(s), purchase order number(s), or by purchase confirmation sequence(s). Although you make this identity to your broker, he is NOT going to make the corresponding identity in his records. Of the 100 shares of XYZ stock that you want sold, your broker is probably handling hundreds of thousands of XYZ shares each day. As a result, the IRS accepts as "adequate designation" your notations in your own records of the specific shares that you are selling. Mental notations do not count. You have to make the notations in *writing*, date them, then preserve them as "proof of designation" when required.

When 100 shares of your XYZ stock are sold, your gross sales proceeds will be $1,250 (100 sh at $12.50/sh). In the 4-purchase tabulation above, which of the 100 shares do you designate? You have three designation choices. You designate each SID choice by marking your purchase confirmation statements.

The simplest designation choice (SID #1) is purchase No. 4. You bought exactly 100 shares at that time, and you sold exactly 100 shares. You made a gain. The amount of gain you realized is $310 (1,250 – 940).

The next simplest designation choice (SID #2) is purchase No. 3. Although you bought 150 shares at that time, it is easy to split off 100 of those shares for a cost basis of $1,050 (100 sh x $10.50/sh). This time, your capital gain is $200 (1,250 – 1,050).

Your third designation choice (SID #3) could be the 50 shares in purchase No. 1 *plus* 50 shares split off from purchase No. 2. Your cost basis in the 100 shares sold is now a tad more complicated. It consists of 50 shares at $8.00 per share ($400) plus 50 shares at $9.60 per share ($480). Your cost basis is $880. This gives you a capital gain of $370 (1,250 – 880). Also note that you have three different capital gains: $310, $200, and $370.

After your designated 100 shares are sold, you have to rearrange your cost basis records for the remaining 275 shares that you still hold. For **each** of the SID choices above, your XYZ "portfolio" would appear as follows:

SID #1

Purchase No. 1	50 sh	@	8.00/sh	=	400
" No. 2	75 sh	@	9.60/sh	=	720
" No. 3	150 sh	@	10.50/sh	=	1,575
" No. 4	<SOLD 100>				-0-
	275 sh				$2,695

SID #2

Purchase No. 1	50 sh	@	8.00/sh	=	400
" No. 2	75 sh	@	9.60/sh	=	720
" No. 3	<SOLD 100>				
	50 sh	@	10.50/sh	=	525
" No. 4	100 sh	@	9.40/sh	=	940
	275 sh				$2,585

SID #3

Purchase No. 1	<SOLD 50>				-0-
" No. 2	<SOLD 50>				
	25 sh	@	9.60/sh	=	240
" No. 3	150 sh	@	10.50/sh	=	1,575
" No. 4	100 sh	@	9.40/sh	=	940
	275 sh				$2,755

As you can see, there are a lot of records readjusting when you sell shares under the SID method of cost basis accounting. Three SID choices is about the practical limit for specific designation of XYZ shares. However, the SID method is preeminently advantageous when you want to achieve a specific amount of gain (or loss) for general tax planning purposes.

The "First-In, First-Out" Method

Suppose, instead of the four purchases of XYZ shares above, you made 15 purchases: Nos. 1 through 15. You've reached the point in your investment program where you want to bail out of the XYZ stock, and invest in another winner. But you don't want to do it all at once. You decide to sell a fixed number of shares — say, 100 — each time the market hits a mini-peak, then turns down (slightly). This is a situation where the first-in, first-out (FIFO) method proves advantageous.

In the FIFO method of cost basis accounting, you sell the shares chronologically in the same order that you purchased them. As each purchased batch is sold, you delete that purchase from your records, recording the sale date alongside of it.

For example, suppose your first five purchases consisted of XYZ shares as follows:

No. 1	50 sh (date) @	6.20/sh	=	$ 310
No. 2	25 sh (date) @	8.10/sh	=	203
No. 3	85 sh (date) @	9.05/sh	=	769
No. 4	30 sh (date) @	8.95/sh	=	268
No. 5	120 sh (date) @	8.90/sh	=	1,068

When selling 100 shares, you would cancel the No. 1 purchase (50 sh) and the No. 2 purchase (25 sh). Those two cancellations make up 75 of the 100 shares that you intended to sell. The other 25 shares come from splitting them off from your No. 3 purchase. Your cost basis in these 25 shares is $226 (25 sh x 9.05/sh). This now leaves 60 shares in your No. 3 purchase, for a cost of $543 (60 sh x 9.05/sh).

Similarly, the next 100 shares sold would consist of the remaining 60 shares of the No. 3 purchase, plus 30 shares of the No. 4 purchase, and 10 shares (60 + 30 + 10 = 100) split off from the No. 5 purchase. This leaves 110 shares in your No. 5 purchase, for a cost of $979 (110 sh x 8.90/sh).

Your third sale of 100 shares would all come from your No. 5 purchase. You would still have 10 shares remaining from the No. 5 purchase, for a cost of $89 (10 sh x 8.90/sh). And so on.

Our suggestion is that, rather than splitting up a purchase batch (as in purchases Nos. 3 and 5 above), you vary the number of shares sold to wipe out each purchase batch in its entirety. Instead of selling 100 shares in each of the three sales above, you sell as follows:

Sale 1 — 75 shares (purchase Nos. 1 and 2 canceled)
Sale 2 — 115 shares (purchase Nos. 3 and 4 canceled)
Sale 3 — 120 shares (purchase No. 5 canceled)

It is always best to make tax-records-life as simple for yourself as possible. Selling shares in the same batch quantities and sequence that you purchased them is relatively easy to track and cross-check.

So much so that, if you do not indicate to your broker and do not so indicate in your records, your choice of the SID (specific identification) method, the IRS requires that you use the FIFO method. Otherwise, your *default basis* is zero.

The "Average Cost" Method

The average cost method for cost basising is simple in concept. For a given share issuer, MNO for example, you add up *all costs* of MNO shares purchased. The term "all costs" includes not only your direct purchases, but also your rollover of distributions and your automatic investments. You tally up the cumulative total costs, and the cumulative total shares. Then *divide* the total cost by the total number of shares, to arrive at an average cost per share.

The average cost method is IRS authorized for mutual fund shares only: **not** for individual stocks that you may' have purchased. This point is made clear in IRS Publication 564: ***Mutual Fund Distributions***. The wording on point is—

> *You may be able to choose to use an average basis to figure your gain or loss when you sell all or part of your shares in a regulated investment company. You make this choice **only if** you acquired the shares at various times and prices, and you left the shares on deposit in an account handled by a custodian or agent who acquires or redeems those shares. Once you elect to use an average basis, you must continue to use it for all accounts in the **same fund**. However, you may use a different method for shares in other funds, even those within the same family of funds.* [Emphasis added.]

The averaging costing concept takes root in the fact that for the "same fund" — could also be "same company" — the acquisition of its shares was made frequently. The concept also presumes that you have a chronological listing of all acquisition dates and cost amounts. You separate the listing at that date which is one year or less from Day 1. The effect would be two holding period batches:

short-term and long-term. Each holding period category is cost averaged on its own. We signify this for you in Figure 4.3.

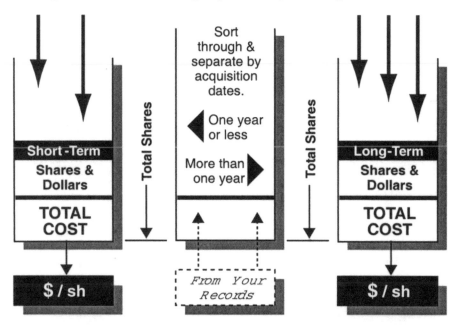

Fig. 4.3 - Cost Averaging Based on Holding Period Categories

The subliminal message in Figure 4.3 is that you do your cost averaging only at time of sale. If there is a period of time between sales, the previous average cost basis will change. This is because the shorter holding period shares will shift into longer holding periods, and new purchases will add to the shorter period shares.

Another way is to "grand average," then apply the FIFO (first-in, first-out) method for holding period categorization.

The "Cumulative Cost" Method

All of the above cost basis methods focus on establishing the cost per share (or other unit) of a capital asset at the time of its sale. In reality, though, it is **not** the cost per unit sold that goes on Schedule D: Column (e). It is your "Cost or other basis" that goes on Schedule D. Stating it another way, it is your *cumulative cost* in whatever you sell. You recover your cumulative costs tax free.

Therefore, our contention is that you should focus more on cumulative costing rather than on unit costing.

Cumulative costing includes not only your initial purchase of a given stock, fund, or commodity, but all of your mini-purchases along the way. Our term "minipurchases" includes your automatic investment pledges, dividend rollovers, reinvestments of capital gains and nontaxable distributions, those stock splits and stock bonuses you might receive, any "stock rights" that you exercise, and any other form of out-of-pocket money that you might assign to a specific stock, mutual fund, or commodity that you are accumulating. Think of the process, if you will, as one selected investment pot into which you dump money into, until you are ready to sell the whole pot. Figure 4.4 is our depiction of the cumulative concept that we have in mind.

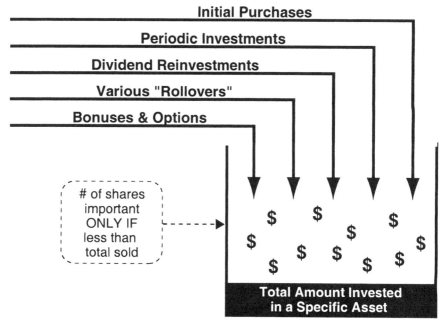

Fig. 4.4 - Concept of Cumulating Costs for "Basis" Purposes

Let us illustrate Figure 4.4 with a numerical example. You put up $10,000 to purchase shares or units in the PQR invesment trust. In addition, you arrange for automatic investments at the rate of

$200 per month ($2,400 per year). You also authorize automatic reinvestments of all dividends, capital gains, and nontaxable distributions. These distributions amount to $400 in year 1, $500 in year 2, and $600 in year 3. Along the way, you exercised (and paid) $2,500 in stock rights offered to you. After three years, you decide to sell all of your holdings in the PQR trust. What is your cumulative cost in your holdings? The cumulative answer is:

- Initial purchase $10,000
- Year 1: 2,400 + 400   2,800
- Year 2: 2,400 + 500   2,900
- Stock rights   2,500
- Year 3: 2,400 + 600   <u>3,000</u>
                                   $21,200

When you sell all of your PQR units, do you really care what the cost per unit is? What if the $21,200 represents 100 shares, 85.692 shares, 135.183 shares, or, after several stock splits, 318.592 shares? Do you really care? Don't you care more about recovering your $21,200 tax free than what the unit share cost is at time of sale? If the gross proceeds amounted to $25,000, your gain would be $3,800 (25,000 − 21,200). If the gross proceeds amounted to $15,000, your loss would be $6,200 (21,200 − 15,000). Whatever the gain or loss, identify your cumulative cost.

Instead of wanting your entire $21,200 back, you only wanted $10,000 back. How would you instruct your broker? Suppose you had 318.592 shares at the time.

Simple. You fraction your cumulative cost, then apply said fraction to the shares on hand. That is, your fraction to sell is—

$$\frac{\$10,000}{\$21,200} = 0.4716$$

0.47156 x 318.592 sh = 150.248 sh

You instruct your broker to sell exactly 150.248 shares. Make sure he confirms this number to you in writing. He should do this at the time he confirms the sales price and proceeds to you. Thereafter, you show your gain or loss on Schedule D relative to $10,000.

The Confusion Caldron: Dividends, Etc.

It is always exciting to make investments: buying selling, exchanging, switching, rolling over, reinvesting, etc. It is fun and a challenge to try to keep the money stream flowing. But it is downright distressing to plow through and reconstruct one's cumulative capital invested in each and every asset issue that is sold. Nothing signifies this distress more aptly than the confusion that arises when automatically reinvesting one's dividends and distributions annually. After doing so for several or more years in a row, one is caught in a *caldron of confusion*. What is the cost basis for an asset selected for sale (or other disposition)?

Adding to the cost basis confusion is trying to make sense out of IRS Form 1099-DIV: ***Dividends and Distributions***. This form — or a substitute for it — sets forth your "distributional proceeds" for the year. When you automatically reinvest these proceeds, you are making a minipurchase of your asset holdings. How do you cost account for these repetitive minipurchases?

First, you need to know what distributive information is reported on Form 1099-DIV. It is all listed for you in Figure 4.5 for tax year 2004. We have renumbered the official boxes and have abbreviated the captions for instructional convenience. As you can see, there are 12 boxes with dollar signs on them. The first four boxes are now quite common. Ordinary dividends (box 1) do not go on Schedule D; boxes 2 and 3 do. Nontaxable distributions (box 4) reduce the cost basis in the assets acquired. Boxes 5, 6, and 7 go on Schedule D but not until its Part III: *Summary*. All capital gain/loss tax computations are made via instructions in Part III of Schedule D.

Instructions to Form 1099-DIV tell you how to report these items on various schedules that attach to your Form 1040 return. If you have instructed your broker to roll over all dividends and distributions, indiscriminately, you have made indistinguishable minipurchases. Do you keep track of these minipurchases year after year? We doubt that you do.

If not, perhaps now you see the wisdom of our cumulative cost basis approach, depicted back in Figure 4.4.

If you follow the official instructions carefully, you can claim a prepayment credit for boxes 8 and 9, and a deduction allowance for box 10. Liquidation distributions (cash and/or noncash) are treated as cash proceeds for involuntarily surrendering your ownership interests when an investment entity is dissolved and terminated.

PAYER'S name, address & zip code	1. $ Ordinary Dividends		**FORM 1099-DIV**	
	2. $ Qualified Dividends		**Dividends & Distributions**	
	3. $ Capital Gain Distributions		4. $ Nontaxable Distributions	
PAYER'S Tax I.D.No.	**DEFINITIVE GAIN**			
RECIPIENT'S Tax I.D.No.	5. $ Sec. 1202 Gain	6. $ Unrecap. 1250 Gain	7. $ Collectibles 28% Gain	
RECIPIENT'S name, address & zip code	8. $ Federal Tax withheld		9. $ Foreign Tax paid	
	10. $ Investment Expenses		Foreign Country	
	Liquidation Distributions			
Acct. No.	11. $ Cash		12. $ Noncash (FMV)	

Fig. 4.5 - Dollar Items Payer Reported on Form 1099 - DIV

For each dividend/distribution rollover/reinvestment you make, you are given a confirming statement by the custodian of your account. Many of these confirming statements themselves are confusing. Therefore, it is imperative that you set up your own records, following our cumulative money method described earlier. Realistically, your sole interest is in recovering, someday, every penny of money that you've invested in every issue of stock or other security that you hold.

Basis Upon Exchange

There are other ways of acquiring an asset than directly purchasing it. One may acquire an item by exchange, by gift, by inheritance, or by abandonment. These other-than-purchases comprise the tax world of "other basis." The implication is that, somewhere along the ownership chain, there was an initial cost basis which has been transformed. The best example of this transformation concept is an exchange.

In the world of capital assets, exchanges of property or rights to property are common occurrences. Exchanges minimize the amount of cash that changes hands. They allow swapping of property forms, debt obligations, and ownership responsibilities. Depending on the circumstances, exchanges may be taxable, partly taxable, or nontaxable.

In a taxable exchange, an owner gives up property worth some value determined by general market conditions. In its place he acquires other property of unlike kind, but of equivalent value. If he reports and pays tax on the transaction, his basis in the property acquired in the exchange is its market value. This is so even if no cash changes hands.

Consider, for example, that owner A had a parcel of land with a cost basis of $10,000. The land is worth $25,000. Owner B wants the land but does not have any cash. He offers A marketable stock and securities worth $25,000. Owner A accepts the stock and securities and conveys to B title to the land. Owner A pays tax on the difference between $25,000 (the "sales price") and his $10,000 cost basis. When he does so, his basis in the new property (stock and securities) is $25,000.

A so-called "nontaxable" exchange is really a misnomer. It is true that at the moment of exchange there is no tax. But at some event downstream, there will be a tax. More appropriately, the term "tax-deferred" applies. Somewhere along the line, a capital transaction will be involved, and tax will apply.

All tax-deferred exchanges have a common ingredient. The primary properties exchanged are *like in kind*. That is, they are "tax like" in kind. For example, raw land for similar land, productive equipment for productive equipment, livestock for livestock (of same sex), commercial diamonds for commercial diamonds, and so on. No gain or loss is recognized (for tax purposes) in like-kind exchanges.

The tax law on point is Section 1031(a). This section, subheaded as **Exchanges Solely in Kind**, reads in part as:

*No gain or loss shall be recognized if property held for productive use in trade or business **or for investment** . . . is* *exchanged solely for property **of a like kind** to be held either for productive use in trade or business or for investment.* [Emphasis added.]

Section 1031(a) says that a like-kind exchange is nontaxable. It says nothing about basis in the property acquired in the exchange. Section 1031(d) addresses this point. In pertinent part, this subsection reads—

If property was acquired on an exchange described in this section . . . then the basis shall be the same as that of the property exchanged, decreased in the amount of any money received by the taxpayer and increased by the amount of gain . . . that was recognized on such exchange.

In other words, in a like-kind exchange, one's basis is simply *transferred* from his old property to his new property, plus or minus certain adjustments. Many taxpayers/investors miss this point altogether. They think that if they acquire property worth $25,000 in exchange for property with a basis of $10,000, their new basis is $25,000. This is incorrect. They merely transfer their old basis to the new, which is $10,000.

Basis Upon Gift

Apart from purchases and exchanges, property may be acquired by gift. In a bona fide gift, full title to property is conveyed from the giver (called: *donor*) to the receiver (called: *donee*) exactly as though a sale or exchange had taken place. The only difference is that no money or money's worth is paid.

The gifting of a single asset may occur in one of three general forms. The transfer may be a full gift 100%. It may be part gift and part sale. Or it may be part gift and part retention, such as in a life estate. Whichever form is involved, it is the gifted portion whose basis upon acquisition must be ascertained.

There is a special rule for determining one's basis in property acquired by gift. It is embodied in Section 1015 of the Internal Revenue Code. It is a complicated rule. The gist is that basis in the hands of the donee is—

(1)   the donor's adjusted basis

OR

(2)   the fair market value

. . . **whichever is lower**.

Usually, but not always, the donor's adjusted basis is lower. This is particularly so if appreciated property is given. The donor's adjusted basis is his acquisition cost, plus additions, less subtractions. Since most donors don't keep track of their tax basis, they leave it up to the donee to figure it out.

If a donee holds onto his gifted property for years, with no intention of selling or exchanging it, he has no basis problem. But if he intends someday to sell it, exchange, or even gift it to someone else, he has to reconstruct its tax basis the best he can. He *can* do this, quite satisfactorily. Doing so means exploring the whole history of the gifted item from its initial purchase (or creation) to the date of gift.

Depending on the nature and value of the gifted item, a professional appraisal may be needed. The appraisal is made both at the time of the gift (its FMV) **and** at the time it was acquired by the donor. For the acquisition time (and place), probing of the donor's recall ability is required. Historical cost records of items of similar nature at the time of the donor's acquisition, constitute valid reference data. Even without a professional appraisal, a donee can establish a reasonable "whichever is lower" tax basis, if diligent exploratory effort is applied.

Basis Upon Inheritance

Property also may be acquired by inheritance. After all of the legal change of ownership and probative aspects are out of the way, the property gets a "new start" tax basis. The rationale for a new start is that all tax adjustments to market value at date of death have been made. Thereafter, the inheritee starts with market value and moves on.

The new start date is prescribed by Section 1014 of the tax code. This section is headed: ***Basis of Property Acquired from a Decedent***. It reads in part as follows:

Except as otherwise provided in this section, the basis of property in the hands of a person acquiring the property from a decedent or to whom the property passed from a decedent shall, if not sold, exchanged, or otherwise disposed of before the decedent's death by such person, be—

(1)   the fair market value of the property at the date of the decedent's death, or . . . [other alternate date].

As you might surmise from the above, basiswise, acquisition by inheritance is more tax favorable than acquisition by gift. Property acquired from a decedent is treated as though it were purchased from the decedent at its market value. This is because, before the passing of title, a transfer tax (death tax) is imposed.

If a decedent's gross estate exceeds $1,000,000 (typically), Form 706: ***U.S. Estate Tax Return*** (for death tax) is required. (Yes, we know that the gross estate amount for the 706 filing increases to $2,000,000 through year 2008.) This form includes various schedules on which the market value (at death or alternate date) is set forth. Information taken from these schedules constitutes an IRS-acceptable tax basis for inherited property. Consequently, if one's inherited property is listed — and fair market valued — on one or more of the Form 706 schedules, he should seek a copy of such schedules for his basis records.

For estates less than $1,000,000, no Form 706 is required. In this case, the recipient of inherited property has to obtain a written appraisal of its value, as of date of decedent's death. There is always some qualified professional person who can furnish such a statement on any kind of property which is potentially marketable.

Substituted Basis Rules

Special — and often complex — basis rules apply to the acquisition of property other than by purchase, exchange, gift, or inheritance. Indeed, there are many acquisition situations for which there are no readily accessible persons, property, or records for basis referencing. As an alternative to accepting zero basis, a substituted basis can be pursued.

The "substitution" of basis is characterized by two approaches, namely—

(1) by reference to the basis in the hands of a like-kind transferor, donor, or grantor, or

(2) by reference to other property held at any time by the person from whom the basis is to be determined.

These two approaches are embodied in the wording of Section 1016(b): ***Substituted Basis***. This subsection reads in full as—

Whenever it appears that the basis of property in the hands of the taxpayer is a substituted basis, then the adjustments provided in subsection (a) shall be made after first making in respect of such substituted basis proper adjustments of a similar nature in respect of the period during which the property was held by the transferor, donor, or grantor, or during which the other property was held by the person for whom the basis is to be determined. A similar rule shall be applied in the case of a series of substituted bases.

The referenced "subsection (a)" consists of 31 adjustment possibilities! The basic rule is Section 1016: ***Adjustments to Basis***.

The whole *substituted* basis concept is to do the best you can to assume a basis that is best like that for the situation you face. Make written notations of your rationale and dollar estimates, but don't rely too heavily on the IRS accepting your figures. Using a substituted basis is always a hard sell. You have to persuade the IRS that no other basis method can be pursued meaningfully.

5

EMPLOYEE STOCK OPTIONS

> Public Corporations May Offer To Employees One Of Three Types Of Stock Options, Namely: (1) NSOs - "Nonqualified" Type, (2) SPPs - "Purchase" Type, Or (3) ISOs - "Incentive" Type. NSOs May Also Be Offered To Consultants And Independent Contractors Because 100% Full Market Value Is Includible In Gross Income At Time Of Exercise. SPPs Require Some Cash Payment At Time Of Grant; Up To 85% Market Value Of Remainder Is Includible In Gross Income Upon Exercise. ISOs Are Structured Primarily For Capital Gain Benefits, As There Are Virtually No Inclusions In Gross Income. ISO Plans Are Highly Confidential.

If you think that trying to cumulatively record your cost basis in the purchase, repurchase, and distribution rollovers of capital stock in a given corporation is confusing, talk to employees who receive stock options. If you are such an employee, you know what we mean. Corporate employers who provide option grants as work inducements flood their employees with complicated descriptions of their option plans. These "plans" are convoluted combinations of (1) Incentive stock options [ISOs], (2) Stock purchase plans [SPPs], and (3) Nonqualified stock options [NSOs]. The chief executives of option-grant companies and their close colleagues prepare these plans primarily for their own financial benefit. They then leave it up to their down-the-line employees to forage through the approximately 7,000 words of Federal Tax Code (IRC Sections 83 and 421-424) to determine what and how to report option sales on their tax returns. It's a holy mess. Most employees wind up paying a double tax: first on their Form W-2 and again on their Schedule D (1040). The Form W-2, recall, is: *Wage and Tax Statement*.

In the great majority of cases, the granting of, exercise of, and sale of employee stock options is includible on Form W-2 as ordinary income. As such, all option amounts so included ADD to one's cost basis in the options exercised. Rarely does any grantor company explain this to its run-of-the-mill employees. Employees, therefore, have to dig these cost amounts out for themselves.

This is where we — and this chapter — come in. We want to explain how you dig out your cost basis from your W-2s. The object in doing so is to enter the cumulative amount properly in column (e): *Cost or other basis*, on Schedule D (1040). The challenge is particularly acute for "same day" sales (the simultaneous exercise and sale). But, first, we need to give you some foundational background.

The Option-Grant Process

Any corporation that offers — or expects to offer — its capital stock to the general public, can also offer certain stock options to its employees. The offer to employees is via an option-grant process whereby the options may be either *given* (at no cost) to key executives, sold (at bargain cost) to ordinary employees, or part given and part sold to designated specialists. The purpose, of course, is to encourage employee dedication to work performance that materially enhances the value of the stock over time.

Granting employees options to acquire stock of the corporation that employs them is a popular form of incentive compensation. The option-grants are generally referred to as *restricted stock*. This is because certain conditions are imposed by the employer before the stock can be sold freely by the grantee (recipient). The restrictions affect the value of the stock in that free transferability (public sale) is dependent upon the employment period of the grantee, employment position, and compliance with other terms of one's employment contract.

All employee stock option plans must be sponsored and approved by the Board of Directors of the corporation granting them. Each "plan" is an agreement whereby an employee has the right, but not the obligation, to purchase corporate shares at a fixed price within a fixed range of dates. In other words, an option "privilege" is extended to one or more separately designated classes of employees.

There are two general classes of stock options, namely: statutory and nonstatutory. The term "statutory" means that two specific tax code sections apply, namely: Section 422 for ISOs and Section 423 for SPPs. We highlight these two sections in Figure 5.1 and also display their adjacent sections on procedural rules. We'll expound on Sections 422 and 423 more fully below. Meanwhile, there is favorable tax treatment when statutory options are sold. The term "favorable" means capital gain treatment rather than ordinary income treatment. Capital gain treatment means not only that lower tax rates apply but also that no social security or medicare taxes apply. Obviously, therefore, statutory stock options are the principal incentives sought by top-level and highly-compensated employees. Lower-level employees must make do with nonstatutory options.

The Meaning of "Nonstatutory"

The term "nonstatutory" means those employee stock options which do **not** qualify for capital gain treatment under Sections 422 and 423. Instead, the options are treated as alternative forms of compensation pursuant to the IRC Section 83. This particular tax code section is titled: *Property Transferred in Connection with Performance of Services*. Here, the term "property" has a much broader reach than stock options alone. It includes any form of property — real, tangible, intangible, or personal — other than money, which had a readily ascertainable fair market value (FMV).

Having a readily ascertainable FMV requires that each option grant be—

(1)   freely transferable by the grantee,
(2)   exercisable immediately and in full when granted,
(3)   without conditions or restrictions affecting its marketability, and
(4)   actively tradable on an established market.

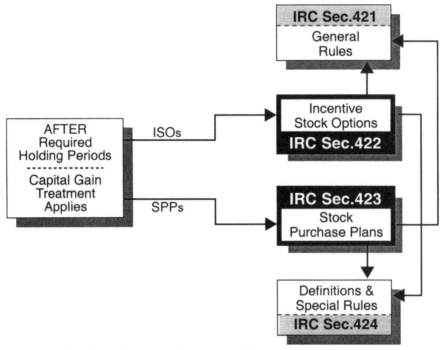

Fig. 5.1 - Display of Employee "Statutory" Stock Options

Because most option grants are formulated as a *privilege* to the grantee, the privilege itself is seldom readily marketable. It is not until the option privilege is *exercised* that the FMV of the offered stock can be ascertained. To exercise (take ownership of) an option, the grantee must either pay out-of-pocket cash or have the full FMV be treated as compensation income. Once compensation income is ascribed, it is treated like any other W-2 income. Social security and medicare tax rates apply . . . as tax add-ons.

The general rule on point is Section 83(a): ***Inclusion in Gross Income***. This tax code subsection reads in part—

> *If, in connection with the performance of services, property* [whether stock options or otherwise] *is transferred to any person . . ., **the excess of—***
>
> > *(1) the fair market value of such property . . . at the first time the rights . . . in such property are transferable*

*or are not subject to a substantial risk of forfeiture
. . . over*

(2)   *the amount (if any) paid for such property,*

shall be included in the gross income *of the person who
performed such services . . .* [etc.]. [Emphasis added.]

The term "any person" means any employee or any nonemplyee
(independent contractor) who performs services for the option-
grantor corporation (or for its affiliate or subsidiary thereto).

Section 83 thus becomes a fallback position for all employee-
type stock options plans that do not expressly qualify under
Sections 422 (for ISOs) and 423 (for SPPs). The fact that this
fallback feature is described by a specific section of the tax code
suggests that the term "nonstatutory" is a misnomer. The more
appropriate realistic term is: *Nonqualified.* Hence, all Section 83
stock options are nonqualified for capital gain treatment when
exercised and subsequently sold.

How Included in Gross Income

Note two particular points in the partial citation of Section
83(a) above. One point — the key — is that the reference for
required inclusion in gross income is: *fair market value . . .* at time
of option exercise. It is not the option-stated value at time of
granting. The option-stated value is to enable grantees to judge for
themselves the market appreciation potential of the grantor's stock,
before exercising their ownership rights.

The second point is: it is the difference between the FMV and
any out-of-pocket cash paid by the grantee that is included in
income. For example, suppose that a grantee paid $5,000 cash for
100 shares of XYZ stock at the option price of $50 per share.
When the option grant is exercised, suppose the FMV is $185 per
share. Unless the grantee can come up with an additional $8,500
in cash [(135 – 50) $ per share x 100 shares], the $8,500 must be
included in income. How is this done?

Answer: In one or both of two ways. For employees, the NSO
(nonqualified stock option) inclusion is entered in Box 1: *Wages,
tips, other compensation* of Form W-2: **Wage and Tax Statement.**

For nonemployees (independent contractors), the NSO inclusion is entered in Box 7: *Nonemployee compensation* of Form 1099-MISC: *Miscellaneous Income*. A thumbnail arrangement of how this all occurs is presented in Figure 5.2.

On an employee's copy of Form W-2, there is an instructional notation marked: "Box 12, Code V." This notation reads—

Income from exercise of nonstatutory [nonqualified] *stock options (included in boxes 1, 3, and 5).*

The box 1 on Form W-2 is wages and other compensation; the box 3 is social security wages; the box 5 is medicare wages. For each of these three boxes there is a corresponding tax withholding box, namely: 2, 4, and 6. In other words, the NSO inclusion amount is subject to all the normal withholdings of any wage or salary paid to an employee.

On a nonemployee's copy of Form 1099-MISC, there is an instructional notation marked: "Box 7." This notation reads in pertinent part—

Generally, payments reported in this box are income from self-employment. Since you received this form rather than Form W-2, the payer may have considered you self-employed and did not withhold social security or medicare taxes. Report self-employment income on Schedule C (Form 1040), and compute the self-employment tax [social security and medicare] *on Schedule SE (Form 1040).*

When NSOs Subsequently Sold

Once an NSO is exercised and its FMV, less cash (if any) paid, is included in gross income, those shares are fully owned by the employee/grantee. The shares then are no different than had they been bought directly on the public market (via a broker). The "cost or other basis" in those shares is their FMV on date of exercise. The "cost basis" portion is the amount of cash paid out-of-pocket. The "other basis" portion is the amount of inclusion in gross income (whether an employee on his W-2 or nonemployee on his 1099-MISC, Box 7).

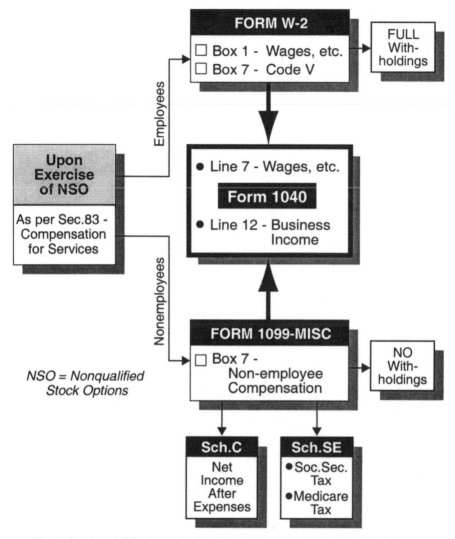

Fig. 5.2 - How NSOs Included in Gross Income of Grantee Recipients

When cash is paid for an NSO, it is presumed that the source of funds for that cash has already been taxed. Similarly for NSO amounts included in gross income. The tax is paid either through withholdings (as an employee) or through self-computation (as a nonemployee). Once tax has been paid on the source of funds from which the NSOs are acquired, the object is to identify those funds and amounts by documenting them. The documented amounts become your tax basis which you hope to recover (when subsequently selling the NSOs that you now own).

A grantee's holding period for an NSO begins the *day after* the NSO is exercised. The grantee can then sell or not sell as he sees fit. If he subsequently sells, the sale is reported on Schedule D (Form 1040) where the respective capital gain or capital loss is computed. The subsequent-to-exercise sale is NOT reported on Form W-2 nor on Form 1099-MISC. We have discussed the features of Schedule D in previous chapters.

A Schedule D basis accounting problem for column (e) [*Cost or other basis*] develops when the NSOs are exercised more or less regularly over multiple years. For each exercise, the FMV differs; for each year, the inclusion in gross income amount differs. And, if the NSOs are held for their capital appreciation potential, their holding periods will differ. Nevertheless, at the end of each calendar year, the grantor corporation provides its version of a statement of account of the dates, number of shares exercised, and FMV amounts paid. Rarely are these grantor statements decipherable by harried recipients when different batches of the NSO stock are subsequently sold.

More often than not, the result is a fallback to the method of "grand averaging" of basis records for completing Schedule D (1040) at time of sale. We discussed our concept of grand averaging back on pages 4-10 through 4-15. We used FIFO (first in, first out) for ascertaining holding periods. To our earlier discussion we add LIFO (last in, first out) for segregating short-term holding from the FIFO long-term holding. We try to synthesize this basis averaging effort for you in Figure 5.3.

NSO Basis for "Same Day" Sales

Rarely does a run-of-the-mill employee (or nonemployee) have the wherewithal to pay cash for his NSO exercises. Nor is he willing to pay tax out-of-pocket on amounts included in gross income, when there are no actual income dollars in hand. As a consequence, most NSO grantees prefer "same day" sales. The intent is that, when a batch of NSOs is granted, the batch is exercised and sold on the same business day by the brokerage firm handling the deal. The benefit is that the employee winds up with net after-tax money, with no capital risk on his own.

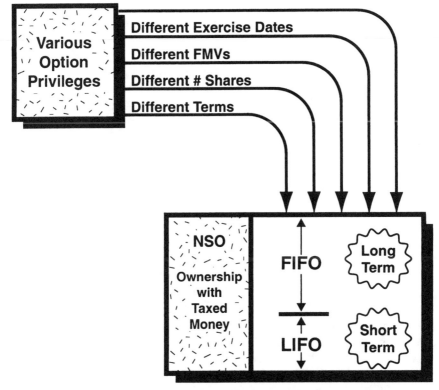

Fig. 5.3 - Basis Averaging When NSOs Not Immediately Sold

For all same-day sales, a unique phenomenon unfolds. Whatever the number of NSO shares sold, the cost basis therein is the FMV on date of sale. There is also an "other basis" element to the extent of the selling broker's commission. Most grantor corporations have a prearranged package deal (contract) with a selected brokerage firm to handle all paperwork, including tax withholdings from the sale proceeds. Let us illustrate the mechanics of the situation with specific dollar figures.

An employee — we'll call him Michael — instructed his employer's accounting office (on company forms) to exercise and same-day sell his 300 eligible NSO shares. The then selling price was $50 per share; the sales commission was 2%. The company directed the broker to withhold 22.35% for federal income tax, 7.65% for social security and medicare tax, and 8% for state income tax (total withholdings 38%: 22.35% + 7.65% + 8%).

What amounts are reported on Schedule D by Michael, and how much money does he pocket?

First, the Schedule D reportings. The column (**d**) of Schedule D is *Sales price*: $15,000 (300 shares x $50/share). The column (**e**) is *Cost or other basis.* The cost basis is $15,000: the full amount of NSO income employer-reported on Michael's Form W-2. The "other basis" component is the selling broker's commission: $300 ($15,000 x 2%). Hence, the column (e) mount is $15,300 ($15,000 + $300). The column (**f**) amount is *Gain or <loss>*: column (d) minus column (e). Thus, the column (f) amount becomes $15,000 – $15,300, or <$300>. The net result is a short-term capital **loss** of $300. This is the selling commission which Michael has to bear, since it was he who instructed the sale.

Do you grasp the uniqueness of the Schedule D situation that we have just presented?

The selling price and Michael's income-reported acquisition cost are identical: $15,000. The $300 selling expense is a capital loss to Michael. ALL same-day NSO sales wind up with this same phenomenon. And with virtually no recordkeeping on a grantee's part. The grantor's broker does it all.

How much cash does Michael net out of the deal?

From the $15,000 gross sale proceeds, the first subtraction is the $300 sales commission. Michael's account is now at $14,700. From this amount, the tax withholdings (38%) on $15,000 come to $5,700 ($15,000 x 38%). Subtracting this $5,700 from $14,700, Michael walks away with a check for $9,000 . . . **after tax**.

For this $9,000 in NSO dollars, Michael risked not one penny of his own capital! Thus, even though a stock option offering is "nonqualified," there **are** significant (after tax) benefits to an ordinary employee.

Qualified Stock Purchase Plans

Going up the employee compensation pecking order a few notches a lower-tiered qualified stock option arrangement emerges.

This is a stock purchase plan (SPP) for designated employees who are not highly compensated. Here "highly compensated" means an annual salary of more than $100,000 or in the top 20% of the compensation rankings. Part-time employees and those with less than two years of service are ineligible. The option purchase plan must restrict the period of time — generally less than five years — within which the grants can be exercised.

Whenever you see the word "qualified" associated with a stock option plan — as an SPP is — additional tax benefits apply that do not apply to nonqualified plans. What are the additional tax benefits? Before answering, we have to acquaint you with the highlights of IRC Section 423: ***Employee Stock Purchase Plans***. Technically, we should be referring to Section 423 plans as ESPPs instead of SPPs. Our use of "SPP" targets the *stock purchase* aspects more directly.

Section 423(a): ***General Rule***, reads in pertinent part as—

*Section 421(a) shall apply with respect to the transfer of a share of stock to an individual pursuant to his **exercise** of an option granted* [under a defined option plan] . . . ***if**—*

> *(1) no disposition of such share is made by him within 2 years after the date of the granting of the option nor 1 year after the transfer of such share to him, **and***

> *(2) at all times during the period beginning with the date of **granting** of the option and ending on the day 3 months before the date of such exercise, he is an employee of the corporation* [etc.] *. . . granting such option.*

The "corporation [etc.]" includes a parent or subsidiary corporation of the option-offering corporation.

What does the above citation mean? We shouldn't answer until we cite paragraph (1) of the lead-in reference to Section 421(a): ***Effect of Qualifying Transfer***. This reference section title alone tells you that Section 423(a) is a "qualifying transfer."

The effect of qualifying transfer is as follows:

If a share of stock is transferred to an individual . . . in respect of which the requirements of section 423(a) are met—

> *(1)* *no income shall result at the time of transfer of such transfer to the individual upon his exercise of the option with respect to such share.*

The statutory language above is an awkward way of saying a key point. The point is that, upon *exercise* of a qualifying SPP, the full FMV of the stock is **not** included in one's W-2 income. Only 85% is included. It is not until the option stock is sold (after the required holding period is met) that the sale proceeds include the remaining 15% FMF on Form W-2. The excess proceeds beyond FMV (at time of exercise) become long-term capital gain on Schedule D (1040). The consequence is that there is a 3-step set of cost-date records to be maintained: (1) grant, (2) exercise, and (3) sale. In Figure 5.4, we try to portray this taxation sequence for you.

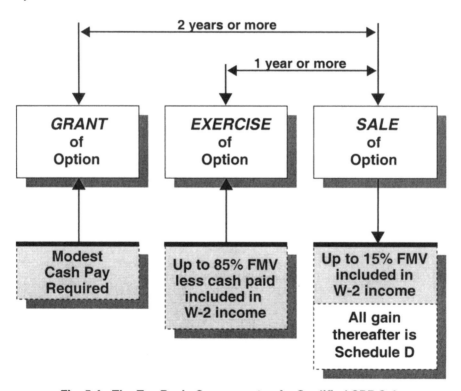

Fig. 5.4 - The Tax Basis Components of a Qualified SPP Sale

SPP Options Must Be Purchased

It is important to note that a qualifying SPP option must be **purchased** by an eligible employee. The purchase price may come from: (1) cash on hand, (2) borrowed money, or (3) other W-2 income. For most SPP option plans, a bargain element in the purchase cost is offered. At time of grant, the bargain element may be set at no less than 85% of the FMV of the employer's stock at time of employee's exercise. This 15% bargain element (100% FMV − 85%) is a statutory inducement to employees to purchase company stock, and virtually assures that there will be some capital gain at time of sale. The purchasing costs become the major portion of one's cost basis in an employer's stock when it is subsequently sold in a qualifying disposition.

There are some limits on the amount of option stock that can be purchased via a Section 423 plan. In most cases, the option grantor (employer) imposes a limit in terms of a percentage of an employee's annual salary. A typical limitation is no more than 15% of such salary. The idea is to limit the amount of employer-sponsored risk by an employee, should the company stock decrease in value over time.

There is also a statutory limit to the annual amount when purchasing SPP stock. Subsection 423(b)(**8**) sets this limit at $25,000 per eligible employee per year. This $25,000 amount is the full FMV of the stock at the time the option is granted. This dollar limitation operates on a cumulative basis for each calendar year in which the option is outstanding. For example, if the grant is a 3-year option and no option portion is exercised in the first calendar year, the employee may purchase up to $50,000 in option stock in the second calendar year. If the 3-year option grant limits the total purchases to $60,000, say, the third year purchase can only be for $10,000 ($60,000 − $50,000).

There is still one more — final — restriction on the amount of SPP stock that can be employee purchased. As per subsection 423(b)(**3**), no employee can purchase and cumulatively possess *5 percent or more* of the total combined voting power or value of all classes of stock of the employer corporation, its parent or subsidiary. **In no event** can such stock ownership exceed "5 percent or more" of the option-offering company. This is a mandatory feature. This means that, if so much as one share reaches the 5% owner threshold, the employee's entire bundle of SPP stock becomes nonqualifying. All FMV above the exercised purchase amount immediately becomes W-2 ordinary income.

For example, a corporation has 100,000 shares of stock issued and outstanding. It grants each eligible SPP employee the right (over time) to purchase 4,999 shares. The option is qualified since, immediately after the offering grant, no employee could own 5% or more of the voting power **or value** of the issuer's stock.

If, however, the option was for 5,000 shares (5,000 ÷ 100,000 = 5%), **no part** of the option would qualify for special tax treatment under Section 423(a). The entire 5,000 shares would revert immediately to NSO stock (nonqualifying).

ISOs: The Exclusive "Golden Plum"

Previously, we pointed out that highly-compensated employees are not eligible for SPP option purchases. Surely, you do not think that the CEOs and top executive brass of offering corporations are being left out of stock option privileges, do you? Of course not. These persons comprise the coveted and exclusive club of ISO (Incentive Stock Option) arrangements. Talk about sweet deals, ISOs are the golden plum.

There are actually two classes of ISO plans: restricted and confidential. The restricted class comprises those arrangements granted to *ordinary* highly-compensated corporate executives: division heads and staff. Their salaries range from $100,000 or more to less than $1,000,000 (1 million). The confidential class of ISOs is directed at *very* highly-compensated corporate brass. Their salaries extend from $1,000,000 or more to as much as $100,000,000 (100 million) per year. ISOs are offered to restricted grantees at an attractively low purchase price, whereas the options to confidential grantees are pure gifts. Gifted options are shrouded in corporate confidentiality and secrecy.

Such highly paid persons — perhaps rightly so — feel that options granted to them provide no incentives whatsoever, if, at time of exercise and sale, any amount is included in gross income. They are already paying Federal income tax at the top compensation rate of 35%. Consequently, their ISO plans are structured to provide pure capital gain treatment only. At time of sale, there is no ordinary income component as there is with SPP option sales. While it is true that some "grant price" may be paid, it is paid out of pocket and not via W-2 inclusions. The grant price is truly "pennies on the dollar."

Enter now, IRC Section 422: *Incentive Stock Options*. Its subsection (a): *In General*, is virtually identical in wording to that of subsection 423(a) for SPP options. That is, the required holding time is more than two years from date of grant, and more than one year after date of exercise. Otherwise, ISOs differ greatly.

At this point, subsection 422 (**d**) is particularly instructive. This subsectional title is: *$100,000 per Year Limitation*. The focus wording of interest is that—

To the extent that the aggregate fair market value, with respect to which [ISOs] . . . are exercisable, . . . exceeds $100,000, such options shall be treated as [nonqualified] options. The fair market value . . . shall be determined as of the time the option . . . is granted.

Whatever the option price is — if any — to the grantee, it becomes his or her cost basis at time of sale. To a corporate executive being paid $1,000,000 or so in salary each year, whether the option price is zero, 10 cents a share, or $1 a share, his/her basis therein is not a significant decision-making factor. It is when the stock price balloons to $10, $20, $50 or more per share that the incentive motivation becomes tantalizing. Even at zero basis, the entire sale proceeds are taxed at only 15%: the Federal long-term capital gains rate.

The Valuation of ISO Options

For the most part, ISO options are created strictly out of thin air. This is because at time of grant, due to restrictive conditions on transferability of the stock, no active publicly-traded market exists. Therefore, any FMV valuation of ISOs is a matter of corporate wizardry and spin.

IRC Section 422(**c**)(1) requires only that a *good faith effort* be made to value the stock. Regulation § 1.422-2(e)(2)(iii) goes on to define "good faith" as that which is set forth by *independent and well-qualified experts.* In our opinion, this is not a reliable valuation standard. Especially so when answering to multi-millionaire corporate executives who stand to make a capital gains killing when the ISOs are sold.

ISO valuations at time of grant are conducted behind closed doors in strict corporate secrecy. Matters taken into account are both lapse and nonlapse conditions. Lapse conditions include salary level, employment position, and continuity of service. Nonlapse conditions include nondisclosure of "company secrets" (patents, market niches, manufacturing processes), noncompetition upon separation from service, and "formula limitations" when disposing of the ISOs. The result, typically, is that restrictive options are valued at a mere 10 cents per share

In contrast, confidential options have no discernible market value at time of grant. This is because they are *gifted* rather than being purchased. The result is that a token 1 cent per share is assigned. Under the $100,000 per year grant limitation rule above, 1 cent a share converts to an offering of 10,000,000 (10 million) shares [10,000,000 sh x $0.01/sh = $100,000]. Confidential shares are not exercisable after 10 years from date of grant. Thus, if an aggressive CEO can keep his position for at least 10 years, he could pull off a 100,000,000 (100 million) share confidential deal. If he sold the shares two years later for $10 per share, he could walk away with a $1,000,000,000 (1 *billion*) bonanza! [100,000,000 sh x $10/sh = $1,000,000,000.] Now you know why confidential ISOs are such choice compensation plums.

6

DIRECT ENTRY TRANSACTIONS

> Good Preparation Is A MUST For Columnar Entries In Part I (Short-Term) And Part II (Long-Term) Of Schedules D And D-1. Part I Is A "Clearing House" Opportunity For Extraneous (Small Proceeds, Nil Gain/Loss) Sales, Regardless Of Holding Period. Part II Is An Opportunity For "Creative Disclosures" Of Errors And Omissions, Return Of Capital, Nominee Sales, Estimated Basis, And "Unable To Identify" Transactions. Column (d): Sales Price, As Broker Reported On Those 1099-Bs, Causes "Tunnel Vision" Focus By The IRS. Save Your Precision Talent And Tax Strategizing For Part II Where The Rates Are Lower.

A "direct entry" transaction is when you, the investor, make all of the six (short-term) and six (long-term) columnar entries on Schedule D (1040): *Capital Gains and Losses*. That is, there are no intermediate schedules or forms that you are required to use, before entering on Schedule D. The only requirement you face is the decision to sell or exchange. After having done so, the burden is on you to extract from your purchase and sales confirmation records the necessary columnar data.

Though cited previously in Chapter 1: Schedule D (1040) Overview, the six columnar entries are—

Col. (a) Description of property
Col. (b) Date acquired
Col. (c) Date sold

Col. (d) Sales price
Col. (e) Cost or other basis
Col. (f) **Gain or <loss>**

Of these six items, the payer reports to the IRS entry information for columns (a), (c), and (d) only. Entries for columns (b), (e), and (f) are up to you.

This columnar data on Schedule D is required only for lines 1/8 and 2/9. Lines 1 and 8, recall, are on page 1 of Schedule D; lines 2 and 9 comprise Schedule(s) D-1, pages 1 and 2, respectively. As to all other entries on Schedule D, we class them as *indirect*. We are not concerned in this chapter with indirect entries of any type.

We focus here strictly on those direct entries on Schedule D that may produce either capital gain or capital loss. We also focus on entering **one transaction at a time**. That is, you do **not** combine or group multiple transactions with the same broker into one entry on Schedule D. There are "short-term" and "long-term" reasons for one transactional entry at a time.

Corral Your 1099-Bs

In preparing for your direct entries onto Schedule D, you have a "first task" to do. You corral into a separate pile all of those Forms 1099-B furnished to you at the end of the year by your brokers and others. Officially, each 1099-B is titled: ***Proceeds from Broker and Barter Exchange Transactions***. In reality, only very few brokers — the "B" for broker(?) — use the official form. Instead, they are allowed to provide you with a *substitute form*. As a result, broker-substitute 1099-Bs appear in various formats and electronic designs. Herein lies your first problem to hurdle. You must cull through and separate out all substitute 1099-B forms and statements. It is a more difficult task than you might think.

Brokerage firms are not too happy with having to provide you with IRS-mandated forms and information. Although they are allowed substitutional prerogatives, they let you know that the information they furnish to you is also being furnished to the IRS. The inference is that it is up to you to deal with the IRS: not they . . . on your behalf. It is up to you to distinguish between each broker's substitute 1099-B and his other substitute 1099s.

Most brokerage firms consolidate all of their IRS-mandated forms into one conglomerate form. The lead-in identity is often substitutionally titled:

Consolidated 1099–INT–DIV–MISC–OID–1099-B

. . . or similar wording and sequence. Your challenge is to forage through those consolidated substitutions looking expressly for only those listings preceded with "1099-B." Pull these out and set them aside. Your ability to do this becomes the true test of your eyesight, mindset, and focus on the task at hand. Brokers don't go out of their way to make the distinctions easy for you. Seldom are bold-printed displays of **1099-B** or **Gross Proceeds** presented. More often, the 1099-B/gross proceeds identity is either in very small print or in monolithic computer font.

Don't even think about what and how to make your entries on Schedule D, until you have exhausted the culling process above. As you pull and set aside each 1099-B, get your highlighting marker and color each "1099-B" conspicuously. You want to be able to identify conclusively what is 1099-B information, and separate it from other 1099 items. If you fail to diagnose what is truly 1099-B, you'll be taxed on the overlooked gross proceeds rather than on each transactional gain or loss.

Count Sales & Tally Proceeds

Having located and set aside your 1099-Bs, sort them out by the number of transactions reported on each. Every broker is supposed to list every transaction individually, regardless of the amount of gross proceeds of each transaction. For example, if you've made 25 transactions during the year with the same broker, his 1099-B will list each of 25 transactions separately. At the end of the list, he displays the grand total of all gross proceeds transacted.

Your job is to go through the various 1099-B statements, sort them out by number of sales (lowest number first, highest number last), then hand-mark each 1099-B for quick identity. For example, the following 1099-B data has been taken from actual tax records of three living taxpayers. This data is not fictitious:

Taxpayer "A" —   7 transactions; $ 57,336 proceeds
Taxpayer "B" — 18 transactions; $546,415 proceeds
Taxpayer "C" — 49 transactions; $254,025 proceeds
              74 sales $857,776

Lest you get the wrong impression from the above, we point out that the 49 transactions in "C" were 49 rollovers of approximately $5,185 each (49 x $5,185 = $254,025). Taxpayer "C" was an avid computer trader who bought and sold online through her broker. She was an assembly line worker. Taxpayer "B" was a technician who exercised and sold (same day) his employee stock options. Taxpayer "A" was a retiree who managed his portfolio conservatively. We've grouped these all together because it is not uncommon for one investor to have 74 (or more) sales or exchanges in a single year.

Why do we want you to sort out your 1099-Bs by sales count? The answer is simple.

By knowing your number of sales, exchanges, and other transactions for the year, you'll get an idea of how many direct entry lines on Schedule D you need. Page 1 of Schedule D accepts only 5 entries in its Part I (short-term), and, likewise, only 5 entries in its Part II (long-term). If you need more than 5 lines, you'll need Schedule D-1: *Continuation Sheet for Schedule D*. Each continuation sheet has 24 entry lines for short-term, and, separately, 24 entry lines for long-term. In the case of 74 transactions as above, one would need as many as three continuation sheets (24 + 24 + 21 = 69) if all were either Part I or Part II transactions. [69 + 5 = 74 total listed above.]

After all transactions are entered on Schedule D, the sales price totals that you report must equal or exceed the grand total amount that your brokers report. We explained this all back in Chapter 3.

Identify by Holding Periods

Before actually making the six Part I and six Part II columnar entries on Schedule D for each of your transactions, you have one more preparatory chore. You have to identify all transactions by their individual holding periods. As previously mentioned, there are two such periods, namely:

- Short-term : 1 year or less [S]
- Borderline : Mixture of short and long, same stock, same sale [M]
- Long-term : More than 1 year [L]

Go through and symbolize each 1099-B transaction with an [S] for short-term, an [M] for borderline, and an [L] for long-term. Then go through and count the number of [S] transactions, the number of [M] transactions, and the number of [L] transactions. Be aware that all [S] items go on Part I of Schedule D AND on Part I of Schedule D-1 (Continuation), if needed. Likewise, be aware that all [L] transactions go on Part II of Schedule D AND on Part II of Schedule D-1. The [M] transactions can be a source of uncertainty and confusion when trade dates are within a few days of the 1-year mark.

The two statutory dates of concern are 1 year or less, and more than 1 year. When within a few holding-period days of 1 year or less or more, check your buy/sell trade dates scrupulously. On this point, the IRS official instructions say—

To figure the holding period, begin counting on the day after you received the property and include the day you disposed of it [as confirmed by your broker].

Broker trade dates are expressly limited to business days when the capital markets are open. For example, if April 15 was the trade date on which you acquired a capital asset, its holding period "day 1" starts on April 16th. If the asset were disposed of on April 15th the following year, the count would be exactly 1 year. This is short-term: 1 year or less. If you disposed of the asset on April 16th, that would be long-term: more than 1 year.

Skip February 29th of leap years, unless you happen to buy or sell on February 29th. If you do, treat February 29th as March 1st, then count as above. Any one day short of a statutory date can trip up your Schedule D entry plans. So, check your trade dates scrupulously.

As a summary of where we are at this point, we present Figure 6.1. The schematic arrangement shown is all preparatory. The more transactions you have, the more entry planning you need. Your challenge is to have the grand total of your short-term and long-term gross proceeds be at least equal to (or greater than) the grand/grand total reported to the IRS by all of your brokers. Always plan to do your short-term entries first. Plan so, whether you have three such entries or 33 . . . or whatever.

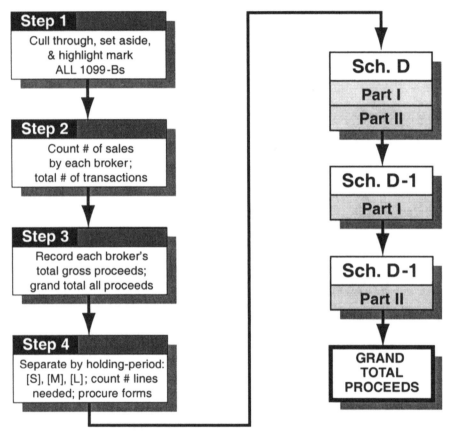

Fig. 6.1 - The Preparatory Steps for Entries on Schedule D(1040)

Short-Term & "Extraneous" Sales

Part I of Schedule D and D-1 (Continuation) is bold-headed: *Short-Term Capital Gains and Losses — Assets Held One Year or Less*. Entries in Part I enjoy no preferential tax rates. Any net gain or net loss in Part I is taxed no differently from your other ordinary sources of income. This fact presents an opportunity to use Part I as a "clearing house" for all short-term, extraneous sale, and small loss activities. By "extraneous sale" we mean any transaction (whether short- or long-term) in which the sale proceeds are $100 or less, or the gain/loss is $100 or less. These nil-type sales cause a lot of entry frustration when trying to be a purist in Part II. Consequently, we urge that you use Part I for all of your small item (called "de minimis") record-clearing chores.

Foremost, enter into Part I all of your nondoubtful short-term sales. Take great care to enter the broker-reported column (d) *Sales price* accurately. Thereafter, use column (e) *Cost or other basis* to include all related buying and selling costs and expenses that you can. In other words, use column (e) for those oddball, low-amount costs that otherwise would get lost between the cracks of the tax laws. Column (e) is your opportunity to avoid always being on the short side of the money equation.

If you have doubts about a transaction being short- or long-term, and the sale proceeds on the gain or loss are $100 or less, call it short-term and enter it in Part I. This is **not** skewing the bottom line Schedule D results in your favor. You are being practical. Actually, brokerage firms do this all the time. Have you ever wondered where those fractional-share sales and remnant proceeds that mysteriously appear on your 1099-Bs come from? The broker is clearing his records of unexplainable, minuscule dollar items. You can do the same.

If you are astute and self-disciplined about it, you can assign all bona fide loss sales to Part I, whether short-term, long-term, or not. Being "disciplined" means assigning only those loss sales which are less than $1,000 per transaction. Loss sales of less than $1,000 are rarely scrutinized by the IRS. There's a practical reason for this. As we'll explain more fully in Chapter 10: Capital Loss Treatment, the maximum net capital loss allowed for any given year is $3,000.

Example Part I Entries

Our view is that Part I of Schedules D and D-1 is an opportunity to clean up your tax records on those matters which add clutter and disharmony to your investment goals. Don't fret over those transactions which are unimportant to the IRS. Make your Schedule D life as simple as possible. After all, any net gain or net loss in Part I provides you with no preferential tax rates whatsoever. Save your precision talent and tax strategizing for Part II.

With the above and below comments in mind, we present in Figure 6.2 how Part I can be used as a "clearing house" for all extraneous activities, including those which are truly short-term. We urge you to take a moment and skim down this figure. It will give you an overview of how Part I can be used, beyond that found in official instructions.

1099-B ENTRIES ON SCHEDULE D, PART I					
Columnar headings as they appear officially					
(a)	(b)	(c)	(d)	(e)	(f)
1 Zebra Corp.	*	*	8,768	6,592	2,176
2 XYZ Fund			5,625	8,936	<3,311>
3 Maturing Bond			10,000	10,000	- 0 -
4 Small Cap Stock			1,250	965	285
5 De Minimis Proceeds			62	50	12
6 Fractional Sale			165	185	<20>
7 Dog A Stock			2,538	3,500	<962>
8 Dog B Stock			4,296	4,292	4
9 Penny Shares			93	100	<7>
10 Straw Sale			2,640	2,640	- 0 -
Col. (d) Total ▶					

* Enter specific date(s) as applicable, especially foreign transactions. Otherwise, enter Var. (various), N/A (not applicable), I/R (irrelevant), or U/K (unknown), as applicable.

Fig. 6.2 - Example "Clearing House" Entries in Part I

Note in Figure 6.2 that we have left column (b): *Date acquired*, blank. For Part I tax purposes, who really cares when you acquired an asset that is disposed of short-term or extraneously? The IRS doesn't care, so long as you report accurately each sales price entry in column (d). If leaving column (b) blank worries you, enter such symbols as: **Var.** (for various), **N/A** (for not applicable) or **U/K** (for unknown). Or you can simply estimate the column (b) date. Then, correspondingly in column (c): *Date sold*, enter month and year only.

Keep in mind that Part I consists of only 6 columns. The 6th column is: *Gain or <Loss> for Entire Year*. Entries in this column should be in rounded numbers, either gain, zero, or loss. The accepted practice is to enter your gain amounts without symbols: not even dollar signs. You enter zero as: – 0 –. The short dash marks before and after the "0" make it clear that no numerical digit has been inadvertently omitted. Above all, if the transactional result is truly zero, **do not** leave column (f) blank. If you do, the IRS will come along and interpret the broker-reported gross proceeds as your column (f) amount.

A loss entry in column (f) is best symbolized by either parentheses (   ) or brackets <   >. We prefer brackets. Some computer-printed entries indicate a loss with a minus sign. Unless the minus sign is clear and bold, it is easily missed. Invariably, the IRS will interpret any fuzzy or flecky minus sign as a gain. Brackets are hard to misinterpret by the IRS. For best clarity, enter all dollar amounts as rounded numbers.

Those Borderline Entry Sales

Many taxpayers agonize needlessly over borderline holding periods and borderline gain/loss amounts. Was the transaction short-term or was it long-term? Did you make a lot of money, or did you lose a lot of money? Enter now what we call the "gut feel" and "coin toss" method of Schedule D entries. We emphasize that such method is **not** IRS authorized, but it is a practical one. It is better to be practical than to go crazy.

Suppose, for example, that you sold 390 shares of MNO stock on the same date. You bought the shares 20 to 50 at a time at various times which totaled about 10 purchases over a year or more. The MNO stock was not very exciting in that its cumulative net gain or net loss was not readily discernible. Now, what do you do? This is a classic borderline case.

First, the "gut feel" approach. As to the 390-share sale, did you make money? Did you lose money? Or, did you break about even? If you made money, did you make over $1,000 or did you make less than $1,000. If you gut-feel that you made more than $1,000, you had better go through, share purchase by share purchase, and determine which are long-term. If this is truly too excruciating for you, a glance back at Chapter 4: Cost or Other Basis, may be helpful. Otherwise, take a deep breath . . . and toss a coin. In fact, toss your coin at least three times. You probably did this anyhow when you bought the MNO stock.

Your first coin toss is: Was there a net gain or a net loss? If a net loss, treat the whole 390-share batch as short-term. Enter the loss amount at whatever your gut feel is, in Part I. Be realistic; don't over guesstimate the amount of loss.

Your second coin toss is: Was there a net gain or a break even? If a break even, treat the 390-share batch as short-term, but show a small amount of gain. By "small" we mean no more than $100 or slightly less.

Your third coin toss is: As a net gain, was it more than $1,000 or less than $1,000? If less than a $1,000 gain, report it in Part I (short-term) using some amount between zero and $1,000. Whatever amount you enter would not be unduly tax burdensome. The IRS tends to question short-term gains less vigorously than long-term gains. Most taxpayers stretch towards long-term gains because of the lower tax rate involved: 15% versus up to 35% for short-term gains.

If your coin toss comes out to be more than $1,000 gain for the 390 shares above, you'll just have to knuckle down and establish the exact amount of long-term.

Where the Action Lies

If you are really and truly seeking to make money, Part II of Schedules D and D-1 is where all of your action should lie. The official caption for Part II, recall, is: *Long-Term Capital Gains and Losses — Assets Held More than One Year*. Because of the preferential tax rates on long-term gains, the correct entry dates and gain/loss amounts are more critical than in Part I. Consequently, you **must be** careful and disciplined in confirming your trade dates and the precision of your records. Unless it is self-evident that your date acquired [column (b)] and date sold [column (c)] are comfortably more than one year, the IRS may question the dates that you enter. This is why the columns (b) and (c) indicate that you enter—

Month — Day — Year (*Mo., day, yr.*)

If you had five or less long-term sale transactions for the year, Schedule D is all you need. But if you had more than five transactions — say 10, 20, 30, or so — it would be better to skip Schedule D and start your entries directly on Part II of Schedule D-1. There you could broker-trade or computer-trade your heart out, all you want. Just keep good tracking records and "batch organize" them as you go along.

Before making any entries on Schedule D-1, batch organize them as follows—

Batch 1 — sale dates within 10 days of 1 year
- the most likely to be questioned by the IRS when there are large gains.

Batch 2 — sales which are comfortably all gain
- your comfort zone is when column (e) [*cost or other basis*] is rock solid.

Batch 3 — sales which are provable large losses
- because losses offset gains, displaying losses when large gains is suspicious.

Batch 4 — sales for which payer errors were made or for which "other adjustments" are required.

Whatever your large number of transactions may be, we suggest that you enter them in blocks of five. That is, you skip every 6th line on Schedule D-1. By skipping every 6th line (leaving it blank), there will be 20 transactions (4 blocks of 5 each) on each D-1 page. It is much easier to count — and cross-check yourself — in blocks of 5s and 20s than in blocks of 4s and 24s. There is no limit to the number of D-1 continuation sheets you can use, so long as they are entry consistent.

In other words, if you are an active investor who wants to strategize with the tax benefits of Part II, you must systematize your entries thereon. Focus on the big picture. Don't bog yourself down with fractional-share sales, negligible-proceeds sales, and other minor adjustments for textbook accounting accuracy. That's what Part I is for. In addition to comfortable gain sales and provable loss sales, Part II may also be used for creative adjustments and disclosures.

Role of "Creativity" in Part II

As with all human endeavors, sooner or later you will encounter errors, omissions, and inconsistencies between your 1099-Bs and your own records. Invariably, there will arise "rough-peg" items that won't fit neatly into those six columns in Part II of Schedule D. For all rough-peg items, we urge the use of Schedule D-1 . . . because of the greater number of lines there.

What do you do when your transactions result in return of capital, sales price errors, 1099-B errors, identity omissions, nominee sales, straw sales, and other miscommunications between your broker, family, and friends? Do you just give up . . . and bear all the burden? Or, do you engage in creative disclosure?

For example, do you know what a "nominee sale" is? It is a sale, exchange, or other disposition that you and several of your friends (or family members) made as co-investors. The pooled investment paid off big. The broker handling the transaction reports it all to the IRS in your name and Tax ID (social security number: SSN). How do you get off the hook for paying tax on your co-investors' capital gains?

Answer: Flip back to Chapter 3, pages 3-16 to 3-18: *Nominee Reportings.* The procedure illustrated on those pages results in each nominee recipient paying his own tax on his share of the pooled amount of gain.

We present below other examples of the need for "creative disclosures" on Schedule D-1. The idea is to assign a clearly defined group of line entries in the mid-portion of Part II for this purpose. Don't try to cover up or disguise what you are doing. Lay it out carefully so that the IRS can see it, if it really wants to.

Real Life Creative Examples

Many investors are genuinely bewildered by all of the 1099-B "exposure" to which they are subjected. They are afraid of making entries on Schedule D (or D-1) that are not expressly covered in official instructions or in their tax software programs. Fear is especially great these days because the IRS is in overdrive to force 85%-plus compliance with its electronic filing demands. Yet, there are, and always will be, real life situations where old-fashioned hand entries on Schedule D serve a valid role. Here are some examples.

Example 1. Often a brokerage firm will cash in a bond (or other debt instrument) for you at its face value. If you paid face value at the time you bought it, and you get face value back, you have neither gain nor loss. It is "return of capital." Yet, the broker reports the face value to the IRS as the sales price. Suppose the amount is $10,000. To satisfy the IRS computer, you show in column (d) the amount of $10,000. You also show in column (e) the amount of $10,000. Then enter "zero" in column (f). In column (a) description, enter: *Return of capital.*

Example 2. You instructed your broker to sell some stock for which you paid $3,000. He makes the sale and sends you a check for $3,469 (net after his commission). Thus, your true gain was $469. When the 1099-B is prepared, the brokerage firm reports the sale amount to the IRS as $4,369. This is an obvious $900 transpositional error (4,369 – 3,469) . . . in your disfavor. You add this $900 error to your $3,000 investment amount by entering $3,900 into column (e). You show the broker reported amount of $4,369 in column (d). Your gain in column (f) is $469 (4,369 – 3,900), which is correct. In column (a) description, enter: *Sales price error <900>.*

Example 3. Your broker makes an acknowledged key punch error. For your transaction, he punched in $10,000 instead of $1,000. After receiving your confirmation statement, you call the broker and the computer corrects the transaction to $1,000. In the meantime, his central clearing office reports $11,000 of 1099-B transactions to the IRS. You paid $2,500 for the product, which means you have a loss of $1,500. On your Schedule D, you report $11,000 in column (d) and $12,500 (11,000 + 1,500) in column (e). Your correct loss in column (f) is $1,500 (12,500 – 11,000). In column (a) description, enter: *1099-B error <10,000>.*

Example 4. At the end of the year, the mutual fund that you're in sent you a 1099-B showing a total of $98,362 in sale/redemption/rollover proceeds. From your records, which you diligently kept, you can only identify $90,300. There is a "missing transaction" of $8,062 (98,362 – 90,300) somewhere. Your records show that you indeed net gained $6,500 "plus" on all of the transactions. In this case, you make two separate entries in column (d). On one line, you enter $90,300 and on the next line immediately below, you enter $8,062. In column (e), corresponding to the $90,300, you enter $83,800 for a column (f) gain of $6,500 (90,300 – 83,800). In column (e), corresponding to the $8,062, you enter a fictitious amount such as $8,000. This will produce a small fictitious gain of $62. (This is the loose change "plus" on the true $6,500 gain.) Correspondingly, in column (a) description, enter: *Unable to identify* for the $8,062 entry. Or, you could try to straighten the matter out with your broker. Good luck! Our method is simpler, faster, . . . and more tax accurate.

None of the above examples are hypothetical. They occur every day in the frenzied world of 1099-B computer tyranny. The idea is to force fit your column (d) entries to whatever is 1099-B reported, right or wrong. Then you make "adequate disclosure" adjustments in columns (a), (e), and (f), as appropriate. You do this because you want to attain the results you know to be true.

7

SPECIAL TREATMENT SALES

Risk-Seeking Investors Are Subject To Special Rules Before Making Transactional Entries In The 6 Columns On Schedule D. Particularly Targeted Are: (1) Wash Sales, (2) Stock For Stock Exchanges, (3) 50% Exclusions Of QSBS Gain, (4) Sale of Residence Gain, (5) Worthless Securities, (6) Certain Foreign Corporation Stock, (7) Short Sales (With Borrowed Stock), (8) Gain Or Loss From Options. However These Transactions Are Broker Reported To The IRS, Special Treatment Takes Priority. In Some Cases, TWO Sequential Entries Are Required, Especially Residence Sales Where The $250,000/$500,000 Exclusion-Of-Gain Rules Apply.

The six columnar entries on Schedules D and D-1 (Parts I and II thereof) are intended primarily for ordinary 1099-B transactions. The "ordinary" aspect is that the buying and selling of stocks, bonds, commodities, mutual funds, and the like, invoke no special rules other than designated holding periods. There are situations, however, where special treatment rules apply, before the proper columnar entries can be made.

To give you an example of what we mean by "special treatment," suppose you bought some stock years ago in a promising new company. The company recently folded; your stock is now worthless. How do you sell a worthless security and get a 1099-B? The answer is: you can't. No broker, dealer, exchanger, financial institution, or other responsible agent carries an inventory of worthless securities. Still, there are ways that you can dispose of a worthless asset, and derive capital loss benefit from it. We'll tell you how in this chapter.

What about a "wash sale"? How is that handled on Schedule D? A wash sale is the selling of a marketable security and buying "substantially identical" securities a short while later. The purpose is to align one's tax basis nearer to current market values. If the sale is at a loss, a 61-day replacement restriction applies. Your broker does not keep track of this, but *you* have to. The special treatment is IRC Section 1091: *Loss from Wash Sales of Stock or Securities*. We want to explain this and other special rules to you.

Altogether, there are about 25 special treatments of capital assets for direct entries on Schedule D. There are "puts" and "calls," short sales, "appreciated position" sales, expired options, small business stock (Sec. 1202), bond OIDs (original issue discounts), ESOP (employee stock option plan) rollovers, foreign corporation stock (Sec. 1248), Section 1256 contracts, sale of home (Sec. 121), . . . and so on. Obviously, we cannot address each and every special situation sale that transpires. But, we'll address the more common ones and those which we believe are more instructive for Schedule D columnar entry purposes.

The Wash Sale Rule

Do you want to make an impression on your investor colleagues? Want to sound sophisticated? Tell them that you've just completed a "wash sale" of 1,000 shares of JKL stock. You paid $6,000 for it and sold it for a $3,600 loss. A couple of weeks later, you bought 1,000 shares of the same stock for $5,000. Ask your colleagues how they would handle this on their Schedules D. Why not log on the Internet and spread your query and sophistication around? Ask if anyone knows the substance of the wash sale rule, Section 1091: *Loss from Wash Sales of Stock or Securities*.

Its subsection (a): *Disallowance*, reads in pertinent part—

*In the case of any loss claimed to have been sustained from any sale of other disposition of stock or securities where it appears that, **within** a period **beginning** 30 days **before** the date of such sale or disposition and **ending** 30 days **after** such date, the* *taxpayer has acquired . . . or has entered into a contract or option to so acquire, **substantially identical stock or securities,** then no deduction shall be allowed* [for the loss sustained]. [Emphasis added.]

This seems clear enough. No loss is allowed . . . at the time of the wash sale. Does this mean that the loss is sacrificed? No, it does not. It means that the loss is transferred to the replacement stock as one's additional cost basis in that stock or other security.

Here's how you enter the above wash sale transaction on your Schedule D:

Col. (a)	Col. (d)	Col. (e)	Col. (f)
1,000 JKL	2,400	6,000	<3,600>
Wash sale	-0-	-0-	3,600

When you are ready to sell your 1,000 replacement shares, your new cost basis becomes $5,000 (actual cost) *plus* $3,600 disallowed loss, for a total of $8,600. Did you get this answer on the Internet or elsewhere? [For refresher purposes, Col. (a) is *Description*; Col. (d) is *Sales price*; Col. (e) is *Cost basis*; and Col. (f) is *Gain or <loss>*.]

If you read Section 1091(a) carefully, there is a 60-day disallowance spread. What happens if you wait 61 days? Answer: Section 1091(a) does **not** apply. Did you know this? Did your Internet pals know this?

What happens if you make a wash sale at a gain instead of a loss? Section 1091(a) does **not** apply.

Stock for Stock Exchange

In these heady days of corporate reorganizations, mergers and acquisitions, and megagoliath enterprises, exchanging of old stock for new stock is a common practice. It avoids a lot of money (billions of dollars) changing hands. In most cases, the shares of new stock are fewer in number than the shares of the old. This necessitates a basis readjustment in the cost per share of the new stock. It also means, usually, some odd number and fractional share amounts being left over. The "leftovers" are cleared by payment in cash, in lieu of issuing new stock. The leftover "sales" are fully tax reportable on Schedule D.

The exchanged stock, however, is treated as a tax-free exchange: not reportable on Schedule D. The more realistic term is "tax deferred" . . . until the acquired new stock is ultimately sold.

The rule on point is Section 1036: *Stock for Stock of Same Corporation*. Its essence is—

No gain or loss shall be recognized if common stock in a corporation is exchanged solely for common stock in the same corporation, or if preferred stock in a corporation is exchanged solely for preferred stock in the same corporation.

This "nonrecognition" rule applies not only to an exchange between a stockholder and a corporation, but also between two individual stockholders with holdings in the same corporation. The concept here is that the exchange must be "wholly in kind." There can be no mixing of common with preferred, no mixing of corporations and their subsidiaries, and no changing of stockholder rights before and after the exchange.

There are real problems with same corporation stock exchanges. The problems arise from basis adjustments in the new stock, qualifying the new stock for its nonrecognition role, and satisfying the tax-free egos of CEOs and their executive entourage. As for ordinary stockholders, corporate attorneys and accountants furnish totally unintelligible conversion instructions. Sophisticated formulas and rationale are supplied. Prestigious opinions are submitted that you best consult your own tax advisor. Unfortunately, independent tax advisors are not privy to the glass dome shenanigans of CEOs posturing for their golden parachutes or their multimillion dollar takeover bonuses: all tax free . . . of course. Top corporate governance in this country often reflects unrestrained greed.

Our position is that, if you are a stockholder in a supergoliath reorganization, bail out while the takeover value of your shares is at a premium. Particularly, if you held the old stock more than one year. Report your gain or loss on Schedule D, then wait until the new stock settles down (if you still want it). As a nonexecutive, you're not going to get any special deal by holding on.

50% Exclusion of Gain: QSBS

If the golden parachutes and unconscionable bonuses of megacorporate CEOs get under your skin, there's a true tax plum out there for you. Assuming you have adequate funds, it is the acquisition and holding of qualified small business stock (QSBS) for five years or more. "What is the plum?" you ask. It is the *50% exclusion of gain* rule of Section 1202.

Specifically, Section 1202 is titled: ***Partial Exclusion for Gain from Certain Small Business Stock.*** This tax code section comprises around 5,000 statutory words, and is formulated into 11 subsections: (a) through (k). The word "certain" in its title means a qualified domestic corporation actively engaged in a productive trade or business whose initial aggregate assets do not exceed $50,000,000 (50 million). The stock in such a QSB must have been acquired after August 10, 1993 by a taxpayer other than a corporation. The stock must be "newly issued" in exchange for money, property, or services. If these qualifications are met, Section 1201(a): ***Exclusion***, states succinctly that—

In the case of a taxpayer other than a corporation, gross income shall not include 50 percent of any gain from the sale or exchange of qualified small business stock held for more than 5 years [by each eligible taxpayer].

Furthermore, you can sell up to $10,000,000 in QSB stock and still be allowed the 50% exclusion of gain. The 50% portion excluded is, equivalently, tax free.

How do you claim the tax-free portion on Schedule D? Suppose you sold 5,000 shares grossing $1,175,000. You paid $175,000 for the shares. You held them well over five years; the holding period is not in question.

The official instructions are not clear. But here's how we think you would do it:

Col. (a)	Col. (d)	Col. (e)	Col. (f)
5,000 QSBS	1,175,000	175,000	1,000,000
Sec. 1202(a)	-0-	-0-	<500,000>

You enter on a separate line "Section 1202(a)" because subsection 1(h)(7): *Tax Imposed on Individuals; Maximum Capital Gains Rate; Section 1202 Gain*, says—

> *For the purposes of this subsection, the term "section 1202 gain" means the excess of—*
> *(A) the gain which would be excluded from gross income under section 1202 but for the percentage limitation in section 1202(a), over,*
> *(B) the gain excluded from gross income under section 1202.*

We show in our example above the excluded amount in brackets. Doing so means that the bracketed amount will be *subtracted* from the actual gain realized.

Sale of Residence

One of — perhaps **the** — most popular special treatment sale rules pertains to the disposition of one's principal residence. For such sales, the term "special treatment" derives from Section 121: *Exclusion of Gain from Sale of Principal Residence*. From this title alone, you could be misled into thinking that all capital gain is excludable when selling your home. Your own sense should tell you that this cannot be. There are certain conditions before any exclusion applies. Once you meet the preconditions, there are real — truly real — benefits involved.

The foremost condition is the holding period. Instead of the traditional "more than one year" holding period, there are **two** holding period rules: (1) more than two years when acquired by purchase or exchange, and (2) more than five years when acquired by tax-free exchange. The basic rule on point is subsection 121(a): *Exclusion*, to wit:

> *Gross income shall not include gains from the sale or exchange of property if, during the 5-year period ending on the date of the sale or exchange, such property has been owned and used by the taxpayer as the taxpayer's principal residence for periods aggregating 2 years or more.*

Subsection 121(d)(11): ***Property Acquired in*** [a Section 1031] ***Exchange*** extends subsection 121(a) to "more than five years" when the former property was held for productive use or for investment. The idea here is to disallow a double exclusionary benefit for the same principal residence . . . within a five-year period (ending on date of sale).

Once the holding period conditions are met, the maximum amount of capital gain exclusion allowed is $250,000 for a single homeowner [Sec. 121(b)(1)]. For married homeowners filing a joint return, the maximum allowable exclusion is $500,000 [Sec. 121(b)(2)]. Note that we use the term "allowable exclusion." This means that if your realized capital gain at time of sale does not reach the maximum allowable, the exclusion is limited to the amount of gain. Let us illustrate with numerical examples.

You bought a home on June 15, 2002 and sold it on September 10, 2008. The sales price was $940,000; your cost or other basis (including improvements and selling expenses) was $315,000. You would report the sale on Schedule D and claim the exclusion in the following manner:

As a single owner

Col. (a)	Col. (d)	Col. (e)	Col. (f)
Sale of Residence	940,000	315,000	625,000
Sec. 121(b)(**1**) Exclusion	——	——	<250,000>
			375,000
			taxable gain

Note that the emphasized (**1**) is for a single owner.

As married filing jointly

Col. (a)	Col. (d)	Col. (e)	Col. (f)
Sale of Residence	940,000	315,000	625,000
Sec. 121(b)(**2**) Exclusion	——	——	<500,000>
			125,000
			taxable gain

Note that the emphasized (**2**) is for joint owners.

Suppose, now, as a single owner, the sales price was $500,000 with the same cost basis of $315,000. How would you claim the exclusion? This way—

Col. (a)	Col. (d)	Col. (e)	Col. (f)
Sale of Residence	500,000	315,000	185,000
Sec. 121(b)(**1**) Exclusion	——	——	<185,000>
			no taxable gain

Suppose, now, that the real estate market in your area was in a deep slump. Instead of the $500,000 above, your home sold for $250,000. Your cost basis was the same $315,000 and you were the single owner. How do you report this situation in Schedule D? You do so as follows—

Col. (a)	Col. (d)	Col. (e)	Col. (f)
Sale of Residence	250,000	315,000	-0-
			Zero

In this case, ordinarily, you would have a capital loss of <$65,000>: 250,000 – 315,000. BUT . . . such a loss is NOT tax recognized. Hence, the zero entry in column (d): ***Gain or <loss>***.

On this "NOT tax recognized" point, Regulation § 1.165-9(a): ***Sale of residential property; Losses not allowed***, says—

A loss sustained on the sale of residential property purchased or constructed by the taxpayer for use as his personal residence and so used by him up to the time of sale is not deductible. [Period!]

Fortunately, most personal residences are sold at a gain. This is a fact trend of long standing, and the reason why the exclusionary benefits of Section 121 are so popular. Except for subsection 121(b)(**3**): ***Application to Only 1 Sale or Exchange Every 2 Years***, there is no limit to the number of exclusionary sales that can be made in a homeownership lifetime.

The 2-year rule above is relaxed when one has to sell his/her/their home by reason of *change of employment, health, or unforeseen circumstances* (subsec. 121(c)(2)(B)). In such case, the exclusion-of-gain amount is proportional to the actual qualifying time in the 2-year period.

Where else in the Internal Revenue Code can you get a better deal than this?

Worthless Securities; Treatment of

Forever reaching for that pot of gold at the end of the tax rainbow can sometimes lead to your possessing worthless stock and securities. If your stock is worthless, the burden of proving so is on you. An entry of zero in column (d): *Sales price*, on Schedule D is not good enough. You must establish with certainty that its fair market value is zero — truly zero. If it can be sold for 1 cent a share, and there is a willing buyer at that price, the stock is not worthless.

Establishing worthlessness requires that you try to sell the stock in an arm's length transaction through regular capital markets. Trying to sell through friends, family members, and affiliated corporations (in which you own 80% of the voting stock) will not pass as "arm's length." If your bona fide attempts to sell prove futile, you need a statement from a broker, dealer, or financial institution that, indeed, no market exists. The statement should reveal, as appropriate, that (1) the issuer of the stock is totally out of business, (2) the stock was canceled upon order by a bankruptcy judge, or (3) the stock was converted to another issue, but the conversion offer date has expired. Proving the worthlessness of a security requires research, which takes time. For capital loss purposes, one has up to seven years to do so. [Sec. 6511(d)(1): *Seven-Year Period of Limitation with Respect to Bad Debts and Worthless Securities.*]

The treatment of worthless securities is cross-referenced in Section 6511(d)(1) to Section 165(g) under the general heading of: *Worthless Securities.* The general rule thereunder reads:

*If any security which is a capital asset becomes worthless during the taxable year, the loss resulting therefrom . . . shall be treated as a loss from the sale or exchange, on the **last day** of the taxable year, of a capital asset. . . . For purposes of this subsection, the term "security" means—*

(A) a share of stock in a corporation;

(B) a right to subscribe for, or to receive, a share of stock in a corporation; or

(C) a bond, debenture, note, or certificate, or other evidence of indebtedness, issued by a corporation or by a government or political subdivision thereof, with interest coupons or in registered form.

Suppose, now, that you paid $5,000 for a stock, bond, or other security more than three years ago. You have *tentatively established* that it is worthless with a statement from an established brokerage firm or financial institution. Being "tentative" is good enough. You can always seek absolute, positive proof later. How do you report this "sale" on Schedule D?

Answer: You enter as follows—

Col. (a)	Col. (c)	Col. (d)	Col. (e)	Col. (f)
Worthless PDQ	12/31/06	-0-	5,000	<5,000>
	[last day of taxable year]			

Note that we used the term "tentatively established." A first statement of arm's length worthlessness would be tentative. We think you need three statements of worthlessness from different sources to assert "definitely established." See Figure 7.1 for an overall summary here.

Related Persons Transactions

Wash sales, worthless securities, and loss-in-value sales constitute valid loss entries on Schedule D (for capital assets). The validity presupposes that the loss transaction takes place "at arm's length" in a free and open market. When the transaction takes place between related persons, there is an air of contrivance and suspicion about the loss. Was the transaction rigged in some manner? Did one party or the other — seller or buyer — get an unintended tax advantage? It is this kind of situation that is addressed by Section 267: *Losses* . . . ***With Respect to***

Transactions Between Related Taxpayers. Section 267 is largely the result of abusiveness within (and between) partnerships and S corporations. To monitor potential abuses, some 14,000 words of regulations have been adopted.

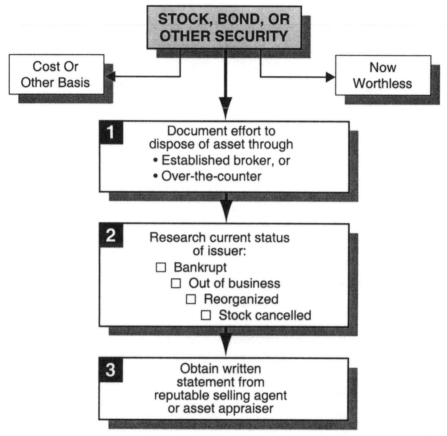

Fig. 7.1 - Establishing the Worthlessness of a Security

The general rule: ***Deduction for Losses Disallowed***, is expressed in subsection 267(a)(1) as—

*No deduction shall be allowed in respect of any loss from the sale or exchange of property, **directly or indirectly**, between persons specified in any of the paragraphs of subsection (b).* [Emphasis added.]

An "indirect" transaction includes a sale through a stock broker or other third-party intermediary. Thus, a loss on the sale of stock through a broker is disallowed on Schedule D if, under a prearranged plan, a person or entity related to the taxpayer buys the same stock that the taxpayer had owned.

The loss disallowance does *not* apply to transfers between spouses incident to divorce, nor to transfers in a complete corporation liquidation.

Subsection 267(b): *Relationships*, comprises 13 paragraphs designating those persons who are related. Included in the 13 paragraphs are—

(1) Members of a family (brother, sister, spouse, ancestor, or lineal descendant);

(2) An individual and a corporation if the individual owns (directly or indirectly) more than 50% in value of the controlling stock;

(4) A grantor (creator) and a fiduciary (trustee) of any trust;

(7) A fiduciary of a trust and a beneficiary of another trust, if the same person is grantor of both trusts;

(13) Except in the case of a sale or exchange in satisfaction of a pecuniary (monetary) bequest, an executor of an estate and a beneficiary of such estate.

You get the idea, don't you? Any property transfer between family members, closely-held entities (corporations, partnerships, trusts, estates), and third-party "prearrangements" are tax suspect. The suspicion is removed only when the transaction is at arm's length. See our depiction in Figure 7.2 as to what the term "arm's length" means.

The no-no ban of Section 267 does not stop at the initial loss transfer. If the loss transferred property is later sold at a gain (by the related recipient: called "transferee"), the gain will be recognized only to the extent that it exceeds the amount of loss previously disallowed. This is the essence of subsection 267(d):

Amount of Gain When Loss Previously Disallowed. You need an example to follow the rationale here.

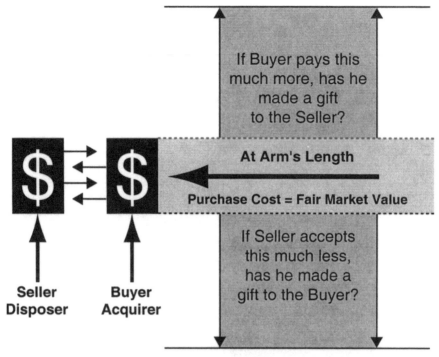

Fig. 7.2 - Concept of Arm's-Length Transaction: Related Persons

A father "sells" to his son an oil lease contract (at a producing well site) for $5,000. The father paid $15,000 for the contract. His $10,000 loss is not claimable on Schedule D. Later, the son sells the oil production contract to an unrelated person for $18,000. Although the son's contrived gain is $13,000 (18,000 – 5,000), his recognized gain for Schedule D purposes is only $3,000 [18,000 – (5,000 + 10,000)]. The son has to absorb the $10,000 disallowed loss of his father. Accordingly, the son enters in column (e): *Cost basis*, the amount of $15,000: **not** his $5,000 actual cost.

Section 267 addresses only "loss sales" between related taxpayers. It does not restrict gain sales. Had the father (above) sold to his son for $20,000, the father would report a $5,000 gain. The son, in turn, would report a $2,000 loss (20,000 – 18,000) re an unrelated person.

Certain Foreign Corporations

Sophisticated investors are fascinated by the prospects of forming their own corporation in a foreign tax haven, and conducting their investment activities there. The belief is that such a corporation, being registered in a foreign jurisdiction, is beyond the reach of the IRS. Such prospects are particularly attractive when the foreign corporate stock is sold at a gain. Before your fantasy gets too far out of line, we must bring to your attention Section 1248: *Gain from Certain Sales or Exchanges of Stock in Certain Foreign Corporations*.

Section 1248 is directed specifically at CFC-type corporations. The letters "CFC" stand for: **C**ontrolled **F**oreign **C**orporation. A CFC is defined as—

Any foreign corporation if more than 50 percent of—

(1) the total combined voting power . . ., or
(2) the total value of the stock of such corporation,

is owned . . ., or is considered owned . . ., by U.S. shareholders on any day during the taxable year of such foreign corporation [Sec. 957(a)]. [Emphasis added.]

The term "considered owned" is defined in Section 958(a)(2): *Stock Ownership through Foreign Entities*. In selected part, this subsection reads—

Stock owned, directly or indirectly, by or for a foreign corporation, foreign partnership, foreign trust, or foreign estate . . . shall be considered as being owned proportionately by its shareholders, partners, or beneficiaries.

The phrase "being owned proportionately" means all ownership interests, directly or indirectly, connected with a U.S. person or entity, down through the chain of multiple corporate interlockings. No matter how ingenious the foreign corporate interlockings may be, if five or fewer U.S. persons have ultimate 50% percent control, the arrangement is deemed a CFC.

Section 1248(a) tightens the noose further. Of its 200-plus words, the key ones are—

If . . . a U.S. person owns . . . or is considered as owning . . . 10 percent or more of the total combined voting power [of a CFC] *at **any time** during the 5-year period ending on the date of sale or exchange . . . then the gain recognized on the sale or exchange of such stock shall be included in the gross income of such person as a **dividend**. . . .* [Emphasis added.]

The message above is that you cannot use a CFC to take advantage of the liberal capital gain rules available in Part II of Schedule D. By recharacterizing your alleged gain as a dividend, you are forced into paying ordinary tax rates on your CFC stock sales or redemptions.

There is a typical strategy when forming a CFC. It goes like this. The controlling owners accumulate investment earnings and profits over a period of several years or more. The profits stay in the corporation as retained liquid assets. The CFC pays the tax haven foreign tax, whatever that might be. On a prearranged schedule, the U.S. shareholders redeem their shares and report their gain on their U.S. returns. The foreign tax paid by the CFC is added, proportionately, to their cost basis.

No Form 1099-B is issued by a U.S. broker. Because of this, a U.S. shareholder has a difficult time establishing on Schedule D the validity of his CFC capital gain. The slightest indication in column (a), *Description*, that a foreign corporation is involved, sets off alarm bells at the IRS's National Computing Center.

If you want to invest in foreign stocks, bonds, or other securities, do so through a U.S. brokerage firm, a U.S. financial institution, or a U.S. mutual fund. All major such agencies have offices or affiliates throughout the world. They adhere to the IRS reporting rules. This aspect alone should make your Schedule D tasks much less suspect, when foreign entity gains or losses are claimed.

Short Sales: Borrowed Stock

For investors seeking more risk excitement, participation in short sales has its proponents. A "short sale" is a contract for the sale of shares of stock or units or property that the seller does not have, or does not wish to transfer. As a consequence of the arrangement, the seller has to *borrow* the stock or other property to be delivered to the buyer. At a later date, the seller purchases "substantially identical" stock or property to that which was borrowed, to cover (and close) the sale. Or, the seller may have previously owned or subsequently purchased similar stock or property, but did not wish to part with it at the earlier date. A short sale is not consummated until the replacement stock or property is delivered to the lender (more often than not, a broker).

Short sales always raise questions concerning whether the resulting gain or loss is short-term or long-term. The *fallback rule* which the IRS uses is: If a gain, it is short-term; if a loss, it is long-term. This does the investor the least amount of tax good. The fallback rule is intended to avoid abuses of short-sale arrangements which are designed to convert short-term gain into long-term gain, or to convert long-term loss into short-term loss.

The tax law on point is Section 1233: ***Gains and Losses from Short Sales***. This is a 2,500-word tax law with many interpretive complications. It consists of eight separate subsections, namely:

(a) Capital assets.
(b) Short-term gains and holding periods.
(c) Certain options to sell.
(d) Long-term losses.
(e) Rules for application of section.
(f) Arbitrage operations in securities
(g) Hedging transactions.
(h) Short sales of property which becomes substantially worthless.

To give you the flavor of the statutory wording, we cite the 50-word preamble, subsection (a). It reads—

*Gain or loss from the short sale of property shall be considered as gain or loss from the sale or exchange of a capital asset **to the extent that** the property, including a commodity future, **used to close** the short sale constitutes a capital asset in the hands of the taxpayer.* [Emphasis added.]

What does this wording mean? It means that the tax treatment of a short sale hinges upon the acquisition, disposition, and holding period of the property borrowed to close the sale. While the sale is open, there is no holding period. One cannot claim a tax benefit on property he may have sold but does not in reality own. Tax code Regulation 1.1233-1(a)(3) puts it more succinctly:

Generally, the period for which a taxpayer holds property delivered to close a short sale determines whether short-term or long-term capital gain or loss results.

The problem for Schedule D filers is the entry dates in columns (b): *Date acquired*, and (c) *Date sold*. Column (b) is the date of acquisition of the borrowed property, **or** the acquisition of substantially identical property to that which is borrowed. It is not a fictitious date that can be pulled out of the air. Column (c) is the date on which the sale is closed, either with the borrowed property or that which is substantially identical. This often leads to date confusion as to whether entries should be made in Part I or Part II of Schedule D.

Our general conclusion is that short sales wind up being bummers for serious-minded investors. Short sales serve primarily as a hedging role for dealers in securities and commodities. Short sales are also used by those in a trade or business who are exposed to unpredictable price fluctuations in currency exchanges, natural resources, and manufactured goods. These persons are not primarily capital gain seekers; they are seeking income and pricing protections in their livelihood business.

Gain or Loss from Options

An option is the right (granted in return for consideration) either to buy or sell property at a stipulated price on or before a specified future date. Usually, an option involves stock or commodities, but it can cover other property such as real estate. Being a right means that the option itself may be treated as a capital asset. Whether a taxpayer has sold an option, or exercised it (took possession) and sold the underlying asset, is a question of fact. Gain or loss from the sale or exchange of an option is considered as gain or loss arising from property that has the same character as the property underlying the option. Thus, an option involves the potential of *two* capital assets: the option itself **and** its underlying property.

Editorial Note: These options are public offerings which are *not* employee stock options of the type covered in Chapter 5.

The tax law on options is covered in Section 1234: *Options to Buy or Sell*, and in Section 1234A: *Gains or Losses from Certain Terminations*. Section 1234A extends the concept of gains and losses on option rights to cancellations, losses, expirations, and other terminations. As always when buying or selling "rights to property," capital gain or loss treatment applies only if the option is a capital asset in the hands of the taxpayer (investor). Short-term or long-term treatment depends solely on how long an option is held before lapsing or expiring.

Because of the "two asset" aspects of options, an investor has added flexibility in structuring his transactions. This is what makes options quite popular. If one wants long-term capital gain treatment on the sale of an asset over which he has an option to purchase, he could sell his option rather than the underlying asset. One could do this and still acquire the underlying asset by exercising the option. The holding period for the underlying asset commences on the date of the option's exercise.

As an investor, one may be a purchaser of an option or a grantor of an option. This distinction is important for Schedule D purposes only when an option lapses or expires. If a purchased option expired, enter the expiration date in column (c): *Date sold*, and write EXPIRED in column (d): *Sales price*. The result is a capital loss in column (f). If a granted option expired, enter the expiration date in column (b): *Date acquired*, and write EXPIRED in column (e): *Cost basis*. The result is a capital gain in column (f). Because an option is a privilege thing, its cost is not great. Neither is its gain or loss, when the option expires.

8

INDIRECT GAIN/LOSS ENTRIES

Gain/Loss Amounts Are Transferred To Schedule D From As Many As 7 "Associated" Forms. These Are: Form 2439 (Undistributed Capital Gains), Form 4684 (Casualty Gains & Losses), Form 4797 (Business Property Sales), Form 6252 (Installment Sales), Form 6781 (Mark-To-Market Contracts), Form 8824 (Like-Kind Exchanges), And Form 1099-DIV (Distributed Capital Gains). A Single Net Short-Term Gain/Loss Amount Enters Into Column (f) Of Part I; Similarly, A Single Net Long-Term Gain/Loss Amount Enters Into Column (f) Of Part II. For Self-Record Purposes, All Of These Forms And Entries Create Verification Challenges.

An indirect entry on Schedule D is one for which the gain/loss amount is computed separately on a Schedule D-designated form. The resulting amount from said form is then transferred to column (f) — *Gain or <loss>* — of Schedule D. The direct-entry columns (a) through (e) are not involved. The equivalent information of these five columns is provided on each designated associate form.

We prefer referencing the transfers as being from an "associated form." That means that each said designated form is a prerequisite to an entry on Schedule D. Altogether, there are seven such forms. Six are preprint-designated on page 1 of Schedule D itself. The directed transfers from these forms go into column (f) in Part I (short-term) and/or into column (f) in Part II (long-term).

In Part I, there is only one line columnar entry for all transfers from all associated forms. Similarly, for Part II (of Schedule D).

This means that each entry is the *net* of several multiple amounts from several associated forms. If you have five associated forms, for example, two might be short-term nets and three might be long-term nets. For record-tracking purposes, this could present a problem. One solution would be to make hand-noted subentries in the available white space on Schedule D, to correspond with each applicable associated form.

In this chapter, therefore, we want to at least acquaint you with all of the associated forms. This necessitates our citing the official form numbers and titles, and our making some comments on each form's general format. We have no intention of trying to make you an expert on said forms. We think only that you should be aware they exist . . . and why they exist. There is more to being a serious-minded investor than just buying and selling stock through a broker. There is a vast world of other Schedule D opportunities out there. Your investment advisor may not know about them . . . nor be interested in them.

Transfer Collection Lines

As indicated above, all directed amounts from the associated forms go onto specifically designated transfer lines on Schedule D. There are two such lines, namely: **line 4** (short-term) and **line 11** (long-term). Each is truly a "collection line." Before an entry is made on either line, one has to collect all transfer amounts from the various applicable forms, segregate them into short-term and long-term holding periods, then gain/loss net them for each holding period. It is the net amount for each holding period that is entered as a single columnar amount in either Part I or Part II, or both, of Schedule D.

It is significant to be aware that neither of the two transfer collection lines (4 or 11) appears on Schedule D-1: Continuation Sheet for Schedule D. It is also significant to be aware that whichever associated forms are required must be prepared either by you or your tax preparer. After such preparation, each applicable form is attached to your return in the sequence indicated at the top right corner of each associated form itself.

The official captions to each of the two transfer collection lines read as follows:

Line 4 — *Short-term gain from Form 6252, and short-term gain or <loss> from Forms 4684, 6781, and 8824.*

Line 11 — *Gain from Form 4797, Part I; long-term gain from Forms 2439 and 6252; and long-term gain or <loss> from Forms 4684, 6781, and 8824.*

Without the detail of these official captions, the two transfer collection lines appear sequentially as depicted in Figure 8.1. Note that each of these lines follows the direct entry total sales price amounts (in bold boxes). It is only the bold-box amounts that the IRS computer sees directly. As to the associated forms, the IRS computer has to address each one separately. This makes more work for the IRS; it makes more work for you also. Your work is greater, because the burden of proof is on you. When preparing each (applicable) associated form, you must do so correctly.

If you have to attach three Forms 6252, for example, and also attach a Form 8824 and a Form 2439, can't you sense the preparational/organizational complexity on your part . . . and the IRS's computer-matching challenge on its part?

As you can note in the two line captions above, there are four forms called for on line 4 and six on line 11. You might also note that four associated forms are common to lines 4 and 11, whereas two forms apply to line 11 only. We list these forms and their official titles as follows:

Common to lines 4 and 11

> **Form 4684:** *Casualties and Thefts*
> **Form 6252:** *Installment Sale Income*
> **Form 6781:** *Gains & Losses from Sec. 1256 Contracts*
> **Form 8824:** *Like-Kind Exchanges*

The line 11-only Forms

> **Form 2439:** *Undistributed Long-Term Capital Gains*
> **Form 4797:** *Sales of Business Property*

Schedule D (Form 1040)	Capital Gains and Losses	
1 2 3	**Part I: Short-Term** Total Direct Sales ▶ ☐	**Col.(f)**
4	Gain/loss from 4 associated forms (see text) ▶	
5 6 7		▨▨▨
8 9 10	**Part II: Long-Term** Total Direct Sales ▶ ☐	**Col.(f)**
11	Gain/loss from 6 associated forms (see text) ▶	
12 13 14 15	Capital gain distributions (1099 DIVs) - - - - - - - - - ▶	——— ▨▨▨

Fig. 8.1 - The Two Indirect Entry Lines on Sch. D for "Associated Forms"

Whichever of these forms is applicable to your case, you and/or your tax preparer have to complete each one, before you can make an entry in column (f) — *Gain or <loss>* — on Schedule D. Similarly for line 13: *Capital gain distributions.* You may have numerous 1099-DIVs to review. Accordingly, it is appropriate that we at least go over the nature and contents of each form. We do so in no particular numerical order other than novelty and instructiveness.

Marked-to-Market Contracts

To start off, we want to introduce you to an unusual associated form. It is common to each of the two collection lines on Schedule D. You'd miss it entirely, unless we point it out to you. It is designed for blue-sky investors who are itching for fast action gains and — yes — fast action losses. It is **Form 6781**. Ever heard of it?

The official title of Form 6781 is: ***Gains and Losses from Section 1256 Contracts and Straddles***. Below this heading, and below your name and Tax ID, you are directed to—

Check applicable boxes (see instructions).

A ☐ *Mixed straddle election*
B ☐ *Straddle-by-straddle identification election*
C ☐ *Mixed straddle account election*
D ☐ *Net section 1256 contracts loss election*

These are elective options that allow one to trim his tax sails on the fast track. If you are interested in further information, get Form 6781 and its instructions.

The Form 6781 title reference to Section 1256 is: ***Contracts Marked to Market***. A "Section 1256 contract" is (i) any regulated futures contract, (ii) any foreign currency contract, (iii) any nonequity option, (iv) any dealer equity option, and (v) any dealer securities futures contract. Subsection 1256(a): ***General Rule***, goes on to say—

*Each section 1256 contract held by the taxpayer at the close of the taxable year **shall be treated as sold** for its fair market value on the last business day of such taxable year (and any gain or loss shall be taken into account for the taxable year) . . . to the extent of **40 percent** [as] **short-term** capital gain or loss, and . . . to the extent of **60 percent** [as] **long-term** capital gain or loss. [Emphasis added.]*

Now, isn't this an intriguing tax concept? Because one is forced to mark-to-market at the end of each year, he is denied the potential of any long-term holding. As compensation for this denial, whatever is the short or long gain or loss character, 60% is deemed long-term, and 40% is deemed short-term. This is known as the "60/40 rule" of Section 1256. Preprinted instructions to this effect appear directly on the most used "Marked to Market" Part I of the form.

The Form 6781 is arranged into three parts, namely:

Part I: Section 1256 Contracts Marked to Market
Part II: Gains and Losses from Straddles
Part III: Unrecognized Gains from Positions Held on Last Day
           of Tax Year

The 60/40 rule applies most directly to Part I of Form 6781. Its two bottom lines read—

- *Short-term capital gain or <loss>. Multiply line 7 by 40%. Enter here and include on the appropriate line on Schedule D, (see instructions).*

- *Long-term capital gain or <loss>. Multiply line 7 by 60%. Enter here and include on the appropriate line on Schedule D, (see instructions).*

The instructions direct you to either or both of the two transfer collection lines on Schedule D.

Form 4684: Casualty Gain or Loss

A casualty or theft is an "other disposition" of a capital asset. The dispositional aspect may be the partial or full severance of ownership and use of property. This can be brought on by fire, storm, disaster, condemnation, or theft. Collectively, these events are referred to as *involuntary conversions*. As such, the inference is that insurance proceeds or other compensation (public assistance, judgment awards) may be available to you. If so, you MUST APPLY for such compensation before you can compute the gain or loss from the casualty. Any and all compensation you receive is treated as the selling price of the property converted. The result may well be a capital gain: not a loss.

The casualty computation of gain or loss goes like this:

Step 1 — *Cost or other basis of property*   _____
Step 2 — *Insurance or other reimbursement*   _____
Step 3 — *Gain from casualty or theft*   _____
         If [step 2] *is more than* [step 1],
         enter difference.

Step 4 — *Loss from casualty or theft*   <_____>
If [step 1] *is more than* [step 2],
enter **smaller** *of such difference
or* [difference] *in FMV* **before**
and **after** *the casualty or theft.*

We've abbreviated the computational steps quite extensively. To do the gain/loss computations right, you need to use Form 4684: **Casualties and Thefts.** Each form accommodates four separate properties subject to the same casualty or theft event. If more than four properties are involved, add "continuation" Form(s) 4684. If there is more than one casualty or theft event in a given taxable year, prepare a separate Form 4684 for each such event.

Form 4684 is arranged in two sections, namely:

Section A — *Personal Use Property*
Section B — *Business & Income-Producing Property*

In both sections, if the amount of insurance or other compensation exceeds the properties' cost or other basis, capital gain results. Section A directs that said gain be transferred to Schedule D. Section B directs that its gain be transferred to Form 4797. (We'll get to Form 4797 shortly below.)

In the event that one's cost or other basis exceeds his insurance or other reimbursement, a casualty loss results. In Section A, before the personal loss is tax recognized, it must exceed 10% of one's AGI (adjusted gross income) for the year. If it does, the net loss amount goes onto Schedule **A** (1040): **not** Schedule D (1040).

In contrast, there is no 10% AGI threshold in Section B. The gains and losses among the several properties are netted. If a net loss results, the loss is transferred either to Form 4797 or Schedule D, as appropriate.

We caution you that Form 4684 is quite complex. In addition to its many small-print instructions on the front and back of the form, there are augmenting instructions comprising some 5,000 words of official text. Consequently, the transferring of capital gain or casualty loss to Schedule A, Schedule D, or Form 4797 often defies common sense. It is as though the IRS were deliberately trying to add to your financial misfortune and pain.

Form 4797: Business Property Sales

If you are an investor engaged in a trade or business, or have income-producing property, Form 4797 is truly unique. Its uniqueness derives from a very special rule known as *capital gain/ordinary loss*. For property held more than one year, any net capital gain goes directly onto Schedule D. Any net capital loss is converted on Form 4797 itself to an **ordinary** loss. An ordinary loss bypasses Schedule D and goes directly onto page 1 of Form 1040. There, it offsets other sources of income . . . without limit. This is unlike a capital loss which is limited to $3,000 per year.

The specific tax law behind Form 4797 is **Section 1231**. It is titled: ***Property Used in the Trade or Business and Involuntary Conversions***. Its essence is—

(1) *If **gains exceed losses** . . . such gains and losses shall be treated as long-term capital gains or long-term capital losses, as the case may be.*

Editorial Note: The phrase "gains exceed losses" pertains only to the 7 columns of direct entry items in Part I of Form 4797. The *indirect* entry items are not included.

---

(2) *If **gains do not exceed losses** . . . such gains and losses shall not be treated as gains and losses from sales or exchanges of capital assets . . . [and] section 1211 shall not apply.*

The reference to Section 1211 is the $3,000 per year net capital loss limitation (which we'll discuss quite fully in Chapter 10).

Form 4797 is titled: ***Sales of Business Property (Also Involuntary Conversions and Recapture Amounts)***. It is arranged into three parts, namely:

Part I   — ***Sales or Exchanges of Property . . . Held More Than 1 Year***

Part II   — ***Ordinary Gains and Losses***

Part III   — ***Gain from Disposition of Recapture Property***

Each part can accommodate up to four property dispositions. Each part also requires (for each of four properties) direct multi-columnar information, similar to that on Schedule D.

Parts I and II accommodate indirect entries from Forms 4684 (above), 6252 (shortly below) and 8824 (further below). Also in the indirect entry category are the recapture amounts from Part III. A "recapture amount" is the *recapture* of previously taken allowances for amortization, depletion, depreciation, conservation measures, intangible drilling, and certain cost-sharing payments. The recapture requirements are mandated by Sections 1245, 1250, 1252, 1254, and 1255 of the IR Code. Form 4797 is not simple by any stretch of imagination. As verification, obtain a copy of Form 4797 (and its 10,000-plus words of instruction) from the IRS or download from *www.irs.gov*.

Rather than trying to display the official format of Form 4797, we present a schematic-use version of it. We do so in Figure 8.2. Our schematic version conveys the general tax concepts more succinctly than the many words of text on the form and in its instructions. Of all forms associated with Schedule D, we believe that Form 4797 is the most important and versatile for those who invest beyond ordinary stock market transactions. Should your "beyond" investments involve bona-fide profit-seeking activities (which are not a sham or not for personal benefit), you can "force fit" them onto Form 4797, whereas you may not be able to do so on Schedule D.

Form 6252: Installment Sales

An installment sale is generally a transaction involving a high sales price. By mutual consent, the seller and buyer agree to transfer the gross proceeds over an extended number of years. A "high sales price" generally means over $100,000. Many such sales by individual investors extend up to as much as $5,000,000 (5 million) or so. Such amounts usually arise from sales of real estate, entire businesses, and intangibles such as goodwill, franchise, patents, licenses (liquor or gun, for example), and covenants not to compete. A special more-than-2-year-holding-period rule applies when installment property is transferred to a related person.

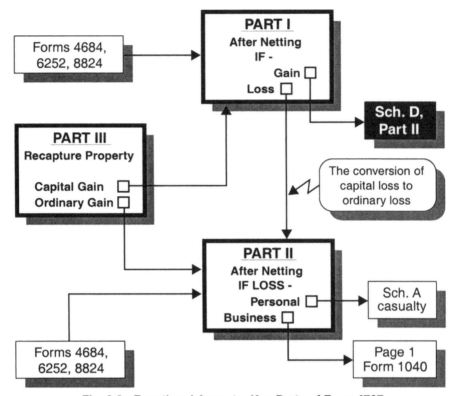

Fig. 8.2 - Functional Aspects: Key Parts of Form 4797

All particulars of each installment sale must be disclosed on Form 6252. This form is titled: *Installment Sale Income*. Its tax law authority derives from Section 453: *Installment Method*. Subsection 453(a) describes the method as—

> *A disposition of property where at least 1 payment is to be received after the close of the taxable year in which the disposition occurs. The term does not include . . . dealer dispositions . . . and inventories of personal property.*

Subsection 453(e) addresses: *Second Dispositions by Related Persons*. Its essence is that—

> *If . . . the second disposition is not more than 2 years after the date of the first disposition, . . . the amount realized . . . at the*

*time of the second disposition shall be treated as received . . .
by the person making the first disposition.*

Form 6252 follows the requirements of Section 453 closely.
Description of the property, date acquired, date sold, and checkbox
questions regarding dispositions to related persons, all appear in
the headpart. Thereafter, the form is arranged into three parts,
namely:

Part I   — *Gross Profit and Contract Price*
Part II   — *Installment Sale Income*
Part III   — *Related Party Installment Sale Income*

The term "income" targets primarily capital gain. Any interest
received along with the payments on principal is excluded. So,
too, is recapture income from Part III of Form 4797.

The crux of Form 6252 lies in its computation of a **Gross
Profit Ratio** (GPR). The form itself uses the term: "Gross profit
percentage." We prefer using GP "ratio" because the multiplier
used is a fraction, such as 0.1234 (rather than 12.34%). You need
at least four decimal place accuracy when dealing with high sales
price items. The GPR is the *Gross profit* (or gross capital gain)
divided by the *Contract price* (or selling price, in most cases).

The GPR is computed from the information in Part I. It then
becomes the first entry in Part II. Once computed, the GPR
remains fixed throughout the life of the installment contract. The
total of each year's payments on principal is multiplied by the
GPR. After subtracting out the recapture income, the net capital
gain is directed onto Schedule D or Form 4797, as appropriate.
See Figure 8.3 for the general effect of Form 6252. It is not
uncommon for an investor to be collecting installment payments
on two or three Forms 6252 simultaneously.

Form 8824: Like-Kind Exchanges

For investors with real estate and business property in their
blood, there is a magic tax-free river running through the IR Code.
It is called: **Section 1031 Exchanges**. This much used section is
titled: *Exchange of Property Held for Productive Use or*

Investment. The concept is that certain types of property can be exchanged, re-exchanged, and re-exchanged again . . . ad infinitum. In the process, little or no capital gain tax is paid at the time of each exchange. In theory, the tax can be postponed until the investor dies. Then, the decedent's estate gets a stepped-up tax basis.

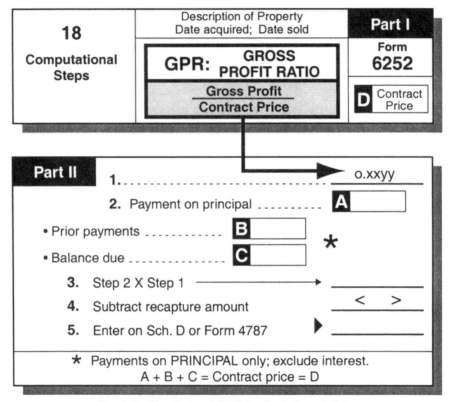

Fig. 8.3 - The Role of GPR for Installment Sales

On this general point, Subsection 1031(a) is instructive. It is titled: ***Nonrecognition of Gain or Loss from Exchanges Solely in Kind***. It reads in key part—

(1)   No gain or loss shall be recognized on the exchange of property held for productive use in a trade or business or for investment, if such property is exchanged solely for

property of like kind which is to be held either for productive use in a trade or business or for an investment.

(2) This subsection shall not apply to any exchange of—

(A) stock in trade or other property held primarily for sale,

(B) stock, bonds, or notes,

(C) other securities or evidences of indebtedness or interest,

(D) interest in a partnership,

(E) certificates of trust or beneficial interests, or

(F) choses in action [chattel or movable items of personal property].

To comply with these exchange requirements, Form 8824: *Like-Kind Exchanges*, is used. This form is organized into three parts, as follows:

Part I — *Information on the Like-Kind Exchange*

Part II — *Related Party Exchange Information*

   • *Can you establish to the satisfaction of the IRS that neither the exchange nor the disposition to the related party had tax avoidance as its principal purpose?*

Part III — *Realized Gain or <Loss>, Recognized Gain, and Basis of Like-Kind Property Received*

The guts of Form 8824 is its Part III. There are 14 computational lines there. Before these lines can be filled in, supplemental computational sheets are required. Supplemental computations involve: (a) separation of nonlike property from like-kind; (b) balancing of equities and FMVs; (c) basis of property conveyed; (d) amount of gain realized; (e) amount of gain tax recognized; and (f) basis of new property acquired. The recognized gain portion, if any, is transferred to Schedule D, Form 4797, or Form 6252, as appropriate.

The very last line in Part III of Form 8824 is—

Basis of like-kind property received.

This starts the tax accounting process all over again.

Form 2439: Undistributed Capital Gains

To avoid a 35% ordinary income tax rate, a regulated investment company (RIC) or a real estate investment trust (REIT) must distribute over 90% of its gains to its shareholders. These required distributions often leave an RIC or REIT short of operating funds. To offset the lack of operating capital, special tax rules permit management to retain a reasonable amount of each shareholder's share of capital gains. Even though retained by management, each shareholder must still report on his Schedule D the *undistributed* amount . . . and pay tax thereon. The law on point is Section 852 for RICs (especially 852(b)(3)(D)) and Section 857 for REITs (especially 857(b)(3)(D)). Both subsections are titled: *Treatment by Shareholders of Undistributed Capital Gains.* The term "treatment" would be more accurate if it were officially identified as: *Taxable Treatment.*

Each corporate management (1120-RIC or 1120-REIT) prepares a Schedule D-like form for establishing its overall net capital gain for the year. The form used is Form 2438: Undistributed Capital Gains Tax Return. Its summary line is: *Net (long-term) capital gain.* Of this net, a management assigned portion is marked for "capital gains distributions" and another portion is marked for "undistributed capital gains." For example, the split could be 70% distributed and 30% undistributed. The management, of course, has to notify each shareholder of his distributed and undistributed amounts.

The notification form for the undistributed capital gain amounts is **Form 2439**. It is titled: *Notice to Shareholder of Undistributed Long-Term Capital Gains.* Its format, as condensed, is presented in Figure 8.4. For your instructional convenience, we have also indicated where the information on

Form 2439 goes onto your Schedule D. The preprinted instruction on **Copy B** of Form 2439 (lower right-hand corner) says—

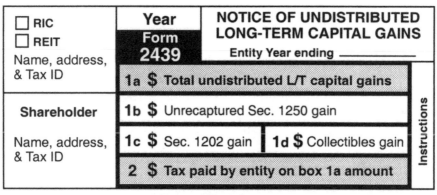

Fig. 8.4 - Abbreviated Form 2439 for Undistributed Capital Gains

Attach to shareholder's income tax return for the tax year that includes the last day of the RIC's or REIT's tax year.

The last day of the RIC's or REIT"s tax year is indicated in the upper right-hand portion of Form 2439.

Do note in Figure 8.4 that there are five $-sign boxes. Each is identified as:

1a — *Total undistributed long-term capital gains*
1b — *Unrecaptured section 1250 gain*
1c — *Section 1202 gain*
1d — *Collectibles (28%) gain*
2 — *Tax paid by the RIC or REIT on the box 1a gains.*

Instructions tell you that the amount in box 2 is a prepayment on your behalf against your total tax for the year. You claim this amount as an *Other payment* in the **Payments** section on page 2 of your Form 1040. Look for the checkbox marked: ☐ Form 2439 on line 69 of the 2004 return.

The amounts in boxes 1a, 1b, 1c, and 1d are required entries on Schedule D. After entering box **1a** on line 11 of Schedule D, instructions tell you to **increase** your cost basis in your RIC or REIT shares by the amount in box 1a less the amount in box 2.

This way, you'll not pay tax a second time when you sell your shares with undistributed capital gains included in the gross proceeds. (We'll explain boxes 1b, 1c, and 1d in Chapter 12.)

Capital Gain Distributions

Unlike Forms 6781, 4684, 4797, 6252, and 8824 which are taxpayer prepared, Form 2439 is prepared by the RIC or REIT management. Similarly, for capital gain distributions. In this case, instead of box 1a on Form 2439 for **un**distributed capital gains, there is a box 2a on Form 1099-DIV for **distributed** capital gains. Whereas Form 2439 has five $-sign boxes thereon, Form 1099-DIV has twelve such boxes. Thus, Form 1099-DIV is a far more comprehensive payer-prepared form than is Form 2439.

Whereas Form 2439 has boxes 1b, 1,c and 1d, Form 1099-DIV has boxes 2b, 2c, and 2d with identical box captions to those on Form 2439. For recall purposes, the captions are:

Form 2439		Form 1099-DIV
box 1b	— *Unrecaptured section 1250 gain*	*box 2b*
box 1c	— *Section 1202 gain*	*box 2c*
box 1d	— *Collectibles (28%) gain*	*box 2d*

As with Form 2439, these items (and others) on Form 1099-DIV comprise part of the tax computational process for Schedule D. We'll cover this entire matter in Chapter 12.

What we really want to get across to you at this point is that both the undistributed capital gains *and* the distributed capital gains are afforded long-term treatment in Part II of Schedule D. But, there is a difference. Whereas, the *undistributed* capital gains go on **line 11**: *Gain from Forms 2439*, etc., the *distributed* capital gains go on **line 13**: *Capital gain distributions.* Line 11, recall, is the column (f) net of all gains and losses from five other forms. This can cause tracing confusion when trying to verify the box 1a amounts on one or more Forms 2439. In contrast, line 13 displays one column (f) tally for all box 2a amounts on all Forms 1099-DIV payer-issued. We highlight these matters for you in Figure 8.5.

We are not sure why there are two separate lines for differently characterized long-term capital gains: undistributed vs. distributed.

It probably has something to do with their legislative origin and the evolutional development of Schedule D. Since both undistributed and distributed capital gains are taxed the same, it would seem more logical to combine them on line 13. Especially since neither type of gain is taxpayer computed.

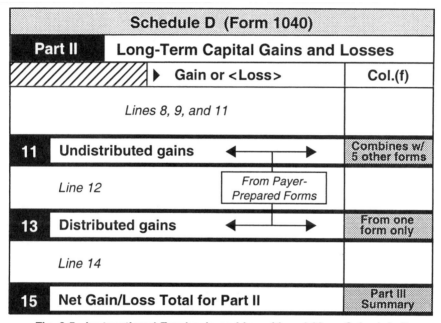

Fig. 8.5 - Instructional Emphasis on Lines 11 and 13 on Schedule D

And, to add a little evolutional intrigue to line 13, there's a new capital-gain-like "kid on the block." It is called: *Qualified dividends.* It is formalized as **box 1b** on Form 1099-B (year 2004 version). We'll address this new form of long-term capital gain distribution quite fully in Chapter 11. Meanwhile, be informed that said distributions are taxed at the same favorable rate as other capital gains on line 13 . . . even though called "dividends."

Hand Notations & Worksheets

Altogether, there are seven Schedule D-associated forms that, if all were applicable, would attach to your annual Form 1040. In numerical order, the seven are: Forms 1099-DIV, 2439, 4684,

4797, 6252, 6781 and 8824. Rarely are more than three of those forms involved in a given year for a given taxpayer. When an installment sale is involved, its Form 6252 may show up year after year. In other cases, there may be two or three versions of the same form. Take Form 2349 (Undistributed gains), for example. You may be a RIC investor, while also being an investor in two separate REITs. What are the pesky chores that lie before you?

Your first chore is to separate the short-term associated forms from the long-term forms. All of the short-term amounts enter onto *one line* — and **one column** — in Part I of Schedule D. The long-term amounts also enter onto *one line* — and **one column** — in Part II. There is an entirely separate entry line (and column) in Part II for capital gain distributions. (Recall Figure 8.1 in this regard.) Each columnar entry, therefore, represents the net gain or net loss from multiple amounts. How do you indicate, at least for your own records, which form each amount came from? There is no provision on Schedule D for this.

If you have no aversions to making hand entries on your copy of Schedule D, we have a simple solution. Hand circle the applicable form number preprinted on Schedule D. Draw a line from your encirclement to whatever free white space you can find on Schedule D. At the end of your hand-drawn line, enter the amount that you transferred from the indicated form.

For example, suppose you had three Forms 6252 for line 11 (long-term). Circle the preprinted "6252" there and show, in the white space immediately below it, *each* of the three transferable amounts. Separating the amounts makes for ease of identity later.

A better example would be Form 1099-DIV for line 13. Suppose the transferable box 2 amounts are, respectively: #1 - 192; #2 - 568; #3 - 28; #4 - 1,720; and #5 - 672. The total entry amount on line 13 would be $3,180. In the ample white space on line 13 itself, hand enter: 192 + 568 + 28 + 1,720 + 672. Neither the IRS's computer (nor yours) can read these hand entries. But you can, should you be IRS challenged to verify the line 13 amount of $3,180.

9

GAIN/LOSS FROM SCHEDULE(S) K-1

There Are 3 Variants Of Schedule K-1 You Should Know About. There Is A Form 1065 Schedule K-1 For Partnerships, A Form 1120S Schedule K-1 For S Corporations, And A Form 1041 Schedule K-1 For Estates & Trusts. Each K-1 Consists Of PASS-THROUGH Tax Information Proportional To Each Recipient's "Financial Interest" (Sharing Percentage) In Each Entity. Included Are Net Short-Term (And/Or Net Long-Term) Capital Gain Or <Loss>. These Items Derive From Each Entity's Own Schedule D (1065, 1120S, or 1041). There Are "Where-To-Enter On Form 1040" Instructions . . . For Each K-1 Recipient.

A Schedule K-1 displays the distributive sharing of income, deductions, and credits among multiple members of a pass-through entity. A pass-through entity is one that pays no income tax by or for itself. Instead, the taxable income, whether ordinary or in the form of capital gains and losses, passes through to individual members. It is the members who pay the tax via their own individual Form 1040s. The amount of taxable pass-through to each member is proportional to his/her/their distributive sharing interests. The tax qualified pass-through entities — often referred to as "K-1 entities" — are partnerships, S corporations, estates, and trusts. Estates and trusts use the same tax forms.

The Schedule D (1040) of each entity member is already formatted for inclusion of the K-1 capital gain/loss information.

Especially for this purpose are lines **5** and **12**. These two lines on Form 1040, Schedule D officially read as—

Line **5** — *Net short-term gain or <loss> from partnerships, S corporations, estates, and trusts from Schedule(s) K-1.*

Line **12** — *Net long-term gain or <loss> from partnerships, S corporations, estates, and trusts from Schedule(s) K-1.*

As you can see, each Schedule D line accommodates multiple K-1 entities. Note the *plurals* in the entity words: partnerships, S corporations, estates, and trusts. This means that where there are multiple gain/loss amounts they have to be combined and netted. Then, if short-term (on line 5), the result is entered as one amount in column (f): **Gain or <loss>.** If long-term (on line 12), the combined amount is also entered in column (f). From this column, all K-1 pass-through amounts combine with all other capital gains and losses that a K-1 recipient may have. Once in column (f) and combined with other column (f) amounts, the origin of the K-1 gain or loss is no longer identifiable.

Accordingly, in this chapter we want to focus on the mechanics of preparing each Schedule K-1, by each type of K-1 entity. Each K-1 entity has its own form of Schedule D, namely: Schedule D (1065) for partnerships; Schedule D (1120S) for S corporations; and Schedule D (1041) for estates and trusts. It is from these entity Schedule Ds that each entity K-1 is prepared for each entity member. A key point for instructional background is that the *manager* of each entity prepares all Schedule K-1s pertinent to that entity. Individual members do not do so; they use their respective K-1s to prepare their own Schedule Ds (Form 1040).

Entity Tax Forms: Overview

Each pass-through entity has its own tax forms to prepare. Before doing so, each entity has to apply for and be assigned (by the IRS) a Tax ID of its own. This ID is officially designated as an *Employer identification number*: EIN. This ID number is comparable to, but differentiated from, an individual's Social Security number: SSN. Hence, when an EIN is used, the IRS expects to see the proper tax form for that entity. This is a prerequisite before any Schedule K-1 is deemed valid.

As pertinent to our discussion in this chapter, the entity tax forms are:

For Partnerships—

Form 1065:	U.S. Return of Partnership Income
Sched. D (1065):	Capital Gains and Losses
Sched. K (1065):	Partners' Distributive Share Items
Sched. K-1 (1065):	Partner's Share of Income, Deductions, Credits, etc.

For S Corporations—

Form 1120S:	U.S. Income Tax Return for an S Corporation
Sched. D (1120S):	Capital Gains and Losses and Built-In Gains
Sched. K (1120S):	Shareholders' Pro Rata Share Items
Sched. K-1 (1120S):	Shareholder's Share of Income, Deductions, Credits, etc.

For Estates and Trusts—

Form 1041:	U.S. Income Tax Return for Estates and Trusts
Sched. D (1041):	Capital Gains and Losses
Sched. K-1 (1041):	Beneficiary's Share of Income, Deductions, Credits, etc.

Now, for an instructional observation from the official forms listed above. Note that the term "income tax" does not appear on Form 1065 for partnerships. The term does appear on Form 1120S for S corporations, and on form 1041 for estates and trusts. A regular partnership pays no income tax whatsoever. All taxable items are passed through, proportionately, to all partners thereof.

In the case of S corporations, there are two items which are taxed at the entity level. There is a tax on *Excess net passive income* and on *Built-in capital gains.* Excess net passive income occurs when the S corporation's passive investment income exceeds 25% of its gross receipts. Built-in capital gains occur when unsold assets in a C corporation are folded into an S corporation under a qualified restructuring plan. The tax rate on each of these two items is a flat 35%. Since the S corporation pays the tax, none of these items pass through to shareholders.

As for estates and trusts, the executor/trustee has some tax/no-tax discretion. He can pass through all of income and capital gains to the beneficiaries. Or, if the beneficiaries are fearful of, or bewildered by, a Schedule K-1, the estate or trust may pay the tax on their behalf. In such case, the entity tax rate ranges from 15% to 35%. At these rates, a slightly higher tax results.

Needless to say, we cease all further comment on the taxation aspects of K-1 entities. From here on, we focus entirely on the origin of entity capital gains and losses and on the arrangements for passing those gains/losses through pro rata to individual members of each type of entity. Let us review partnerships first.

Partnership Schedules D and K

Partnerships are a very common form of pooling money for carrying on one or more active trades or businesses. Though there is no limit to the number of partners that can contribute money, when the count reaches 100 or more, more stringent regulatory oversight rules apply. Partners can be individuals, corporations, other partnerships, estates/trusts, nominees, and others. Each partner expects some form of return on his money invested. One form of return (of money) arises from a partnership's Schedule D.

The Schedule D (Form 1065) of a partnership, relative to a Schedule D (Form 1040), is more simplified. Yes, it has a Part I (short-term) and a Part II (long-term). In each part there are direct entry lines, each with six columns (a) through (f). The direct entry columnar headings are identical to those on Schedule D (1040). Column (f), recall, is: *Gain or <loss>.* Subtract (e) from (d).

One of the noticeable differences in Schedule D (1065) is that there are no official continuation sheets for the direct entry items.

That is, there is no Schedule D-1 (1065) as there is for Schedule D-1 (1040). The reason is that a partnership is supposed to be in an active trade or business seeking, primarily, ordinary income. It is not supposed to be an active investor seeking capital gains. Hence, fewer direct entry lines are needed on its Schedule D.

As for indirect entry items, which have only a column (f), there are fewer of said lines also. There are separate indirect entry lines for installment sales of capital assets (Forms 6252), like-kind property exchanges (Forms 8824), and gain/loss transactions with other partnerships. Part II differs from Part I in that it has a separate column (f) line for: *Capital gain distributions.*

What makes Schedule D (1065) so different from Schedule D (1040) is the "bottom line" (summary) in each of its Parts I and II. The Part I summary line reads:

> **Net short-term capital gain or <loss>.** *Enter here and on Form 1065, Schedule K . . . .*

Similarly for Part II which reads:

> **Net long-term capital gain or <loss>.** *Enter here and on Form 1065 Schedule K . . . .*

Hmm! The partnership Schedule D information goes onto a Schedule K, NOT onto Schedule K-1. Why so?

A Schedule K, unlike a Schedule K-1, summarizes **all** activities of the partnership. There are 46 entry lines on Schedule K, followed by an analysis of the net income or loss by partner type and class. The Schedule K, therefore, is an internal financial document for gauging management's success or nonsuccess. Attention for analysis focuses primarily on the **Income <Loss>** portion of the Schedule K. A digest of this portion is presented in Figure 9.1. Be aware that items 8 and 9 derive directly from Schedule D (Form 1065).

Schedule K-1 (Form 1065)

Itemwise and linewise, Part III of Schedule K-1 (Form 1065) is virtually an exact match with those items and lines on Schedule K of Form 1065. The key difference is that Schedule K pertains to all partners collectively, whereas Schedule K-1 pertains to each partner individually.

Form 1065	Partners' Distributive Share Items	Sch. K
Item	Attach required associated forms	Amount
1	Ordinary business income / <loss>	
2	Net rental real estate income / <loss>	
3	Other net rental income / <loss>	
4	Guaranteed payments	
5	Interest income	
6	Dividends: Ordinary _____ Qualified ▨▨▨	▨▨▨
7	Royalties	
8	**Net short-term capital gain / <loss>**	
9	**Net long-term capital gain / <loss>**	
10	▨▨ Collectibles (28%) gain / <loss> ▨▨	▨▨
11	▨▨ Unrecaptured Sec. 1250 gain ▨▨	▨▨
12	Net Section 1231 gain / <loss> (Form 4797)	
13	Other income / <loss> (attach statement)	
▨▨	*Many other distributive share items*	▨▨

Fig. 9.1 - The Income / <Loss> Items on a Partnership Schedule K

The number of K-1s prepared and attached to Form 1065 is indicated at the head portion of Form 1065. There's a long line there which reads—

Number of Schedules K-1. Attach one for each person who was a partner **at any time** *during the tax year* ▶ _____.

Schedule K-1 also differs from Schedule K in that there is a Part I and Part II, as well as Part III. The official captions to these parts are:

Part I   — Information about the Partnership
Part II   — Information about the Partner
Part III   — Partner's Share of . . . Items

In abbreviated form, the general arrangement of a Schedule K-1 (1065) is presented in Figure 9.2. It is essentially two full-length sheets of information on one page.

Schedule K-1 (Form 1065)	Part III	Partner's Share of
Partner's Share of Income, etc.		**. . . Current Year Items**
Part I Info About Partnership		*See back of form for "where-to-enter" on your Form 1040*
• EIN • Name & address • IRS Center where partnership filed return _____	Income/<Loss> [See Fig. 9.1] **8.** Net short-term capital gain / <loss>	Credits, etc. Foreign transactions
Part II Info About Partner • SSN • Name & address • Type of Partner ☐ ☐ ☐ ☐ **L.** Partner's share of profit, loss, & capital. _____ _____	**9.** Net long-term capital gain / <loss>	Alternative minimum tax items
M. Partner's share of liabilities at year end. _____ _____	Deductions	Tax-exempt income
	Self-Employment Earnings	Distributions
N. Partner's capital account analysis. _____ _____		Other information
	For IRS Use Only	

Fig. 9.2 - Abbreviated Format of Schedule K-1 for a Partnership

In Part I, the EIN of the partnership is the first entry there. This is followed by the partnership's name and address, and the IRS center where the partnership's return (Form 1065 with all K-1s attached) was filed. Thus, the IRS knows promptly if a Schedule K-1 has been issued in your name, address, and Tax ID (SSN if individual; EIN if entity).

In Part II, there are checkboxes for indicating the type of partner you are:

☐ *General,* ☐ *Limited,* ☐ *Domestic,* or ☐ *Foreign*

These checkboxes are followed by the designation of your status as an individual or an entity. This designation is followed by an alphabetized line "L", captioned as—

Partner's share of profit, loss, and capital:

• ***Beginning*_____*%; Ending*_____*%.***

It is a partner's capital percentage at the end of the partnership's accounting period that determines the pass-through amount of capital gains and losses. For example, suppose your "capital percentage ending" was 2.16% (0.0216). And further suppose that the partnership's Schedule K net long-term capital gain was $185,185. Your pass-through capital gain would be $4,000 [185,185 x 0.0216].

Editorial Note: · Most partnerships operate on a fiscal year basis, whereas most individual partners operate on a calendar year basis. This accounting year misfit can cause computer mismatching notices from the IRS. To avert such mismatchings, the partnership is IRS instructed to use the Schedule K-1 with the tax year preprinted thereon that corresponds with the Form 1040 calendar year.

We also want to comment on lines M and N on the Schedule K-1 (1065). Line "M" is captioned—

Partner's share of liabilities at year end.

The term "liabilities" refers to the amount of borrowed money, instead of cash money and property that went into the partnership on behalf of a partner. The line "N" is captioned—

Partner's capital account analysis.

This line consists of specific dollar amount entries for: (a) *Beginning capital,* (b) Capital contributed, (c) Current year increase/<decrease>, (d) Withdrawals and distributions, and (e) *Ending capital.* The terms "beginning" and "ending" refer to the partnership's accounting year. Such year could end on April 30, June 30, or September 30, rather than on December 31.

So, when a Schedule K-1 (1065) is issued to you in your name and SSN, you want to check carefully its lines L, M, and N in Part II. This is your risk capital that is on the line for partnership activities. Suppose your ending risk capital is $3,500, for example, and the K-1 shows your share of the partnership loss to be $9,000. Your allowable loss pass-through is $3,500; it is not $9,000. You can never write off more than the true amount of your economic risk. You are *at-risk limited* regardless of the nature of the pass-through loss (IRC Sec. 469: Passive Activity Losses . . . Limited).

Part III, Schedule K-1 (1065)

For pass-through tax purposes, Part III of your Schedule K-1 (1065) is where the action lies. Its full caption reads—

Partner's Share of Current Year Income, Deductions, Credits, and Other Items

▶ *See back of form and separate instructions.*

The back side of Part III is designated as page 2 of the K-1. On this page are listed approximately 100 items, each with line numbers and alphabetic codes. The headnote to page 2 reads:

This list identifies the codes used on Schedule K-1 for all partners and provides summarized reporting information for partners who file Form 1040.

By simply glancing at page 2 of your Schedule K-1 (Form 1065) — you need an official copy for this glancing — you can sense the immense diversity of partnership investment activities.

No wonder so many individual investors participate as "limited partners" in a responsible partnership.

The front side of Part III (page 1) shows the dollar amounts of each item to which you are pass-through entitled. Although some 20 captioned lines are preprinted on page 1 (many with additional blank lines: recall Figure 9.2), probably not more than a half dozen or so affect you. As pertinent to the subject of this chapter, there are only two lines of interest. They are—

- *Net short-term capital gain/ <loss>*

- *Net long-term capital gain/<loss>*

What does page 2 say about these two page 1 pass-through amounts?

For the net short-term amount, it says:

Enter on Schedule D (1040), line 5, column (f)

Similarly, for the net long-term amount, it says:

Enter on Schedule D (1040), line 12, column (f)

The column (f) of lines 5/12 on your own Schedule D corresponds exactly with the Part III, Schedule K-1, item headings above. The same item words on your Schedule D are followed by—

. . . from partnerships, S corporations, estates, and trusts from Schedule(s) K-1.

To put the above matters in perspective for you, we present Figure 9.3. Note that we start with your invested money and follow its trail through the "partnership maze." The end result we hope is at least some net long-term capital gain.

S Corporation Schedules D, K, & K-1

As pass-through investment entities, S corporations and partnerships have much in common. From a purely investment point of view, S corporations require more active attention because fewer participants are involved. An S corporation is primarily a business run for livelihood purposes, more so than is a partnership. A partnership engages in risk-taking entrepreneurial activities which may pay off big . . . or lose big.

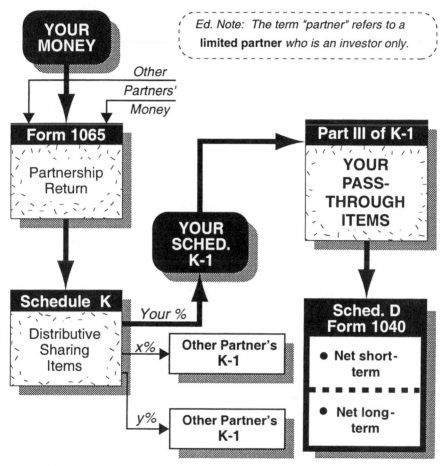

Fig. 9.3 - An Investor's "Money Trail" Through a Partnership

The livelihood interests in a partnership are the general partners who perform day-to-day operations on behalf of the limited partners. The general partners are paid a salary, called: *Guaranteed payments*, but put up only about 5% of the operating capital needed. The limited partners put up about 95% of said capital. In contrast, the officers of an S corporation and their close friends put up at least 51% of the capital needed (for control purposes), then invite others (called: minority shareholders) to contribute the rest.

Nevertheless, an S corporation is a pass-through entity with its own Schedules D, K, and K-1. While not exactly identical to the corresponding partnership schedules, they are very similar. For example, whereas a partnership Schedule D has a Part I and a Part II, the S corporation Schedule D has a Part III (for built-in capital gains). As explained previously, the 35% built-in gains tax is borne solely by the corporation and none is passed through. Otherwise, the bottom lines on Parts I and II are word identical. It is the transference to Schedule K where line numbers differ.

With respect to an S corporation's Schedule D (1120S) gain/loss nets, they are routed through to identically captioned lines on Schedule K (1120S) and Schedule K-1 (1120S). This is why we spent the instructive time we did on partnership Schedules D, K, and K-1. The S corporation aspects are nearly identical. Recall Figures 9.1, 9.2, and 9.3 in this regard.

The only noticeable difference between the K-1 for an S corporation and that for a partnership is the Part II thereof. The Part II (***Information about Shareholder***) of an S corporation K-1 displays only three line captions. These are—

- *Shareholder's* [tax] *identifying number,*
- *Shareholder's name and address, and*
- *Shareholder's percentage of stock ownership for* [entire] *tax year . . ._____%.*

This one-liner percentage item on a K-1 (1120S) contrasts with 11 lines (3 in %s and 8 in $s) on a partnership K-1. In other words, figuring the pro rata distributive sharing interest in an S corporation is simpler than that in a partnership.

Estates and Trusts Commentary

There is a vast functional difference between partnerships and S corporations, and estates or trusts. Whereas a partnership or S corporation is a contributory entity, an estate or trust is purely a distributing entity. What's the difference? One difference is that you cannot put money into an estate or trust, like you can with a partnership or S corporation. In an estate or trust, you are a *beneficiary* of someone else's money and assets after that person has predeceased you. An estate or trust is not engaged in ongoing entrepreneurial objectives the way a partnership or S corporation does business. You benefit from someone else's entrepreneurial objectives: not from your own.

Yes, there are pension trusts, annuity trusts, insurance trusts, etc. where you put money in . . . and get money out under a contractual plan. These are classed as business trusts. When money comes out on your behalf, you are issued a **Form 1099-R**. Its title is: ***Distributions from Pensions, Annuities, Retirement or Profit-Sharing Plans, IRAs, Insurance Contracts, etc.*** There are no business estates other than bankruptcy estates, which issue no 1099-Rs. Since the focus of this chapter is on Schedules K-1, the only estates and trusts that issue K-1s are personal and family inheritances.

As listed earlier, the initial document of an estate or trust is Form 1041: ***U.S. Income Tax Return for Estates and Trusts***. For best understanding of the role of Form 1041, think of it as an **inheritance entity**. It requires an EIN, date of creation, designation of type, and a headblock which asks for—

Number of Schedules K-1 attached  _____

An estate and a trust are different functional entities. For this reason, a separate EIN is required for each. An estate has short-term duration, whereas a trust may be longer term. A statement at the bottom of page 2 of Form 1041 asks—

If decedent's estate has been open for more than 2 years, attach an explanation for delay in closing estate, and check here ► ☐.

In substance, an estate is a one-time distribution of a decedent's assets, whereas a trust may distribute the same assets over multiple years. Until all assets of a decedent and/or his spouse are distributed to his/her/their designated beneficiaries, the estate or trust may generate income from those assets. Hence, the need for Form 1041.

Schedule D (Form 1041)

Not being an entrepreneurial entity, there is no Schedule K for an estate or trust. Information from Schedule D goes directly onto Schedule K-1 . . . with a twist. The "twist" is that the fiduciary (executor of an estate; trustee of a trust) has some discretion as to how much of the Schedule D benefits (net capital gain) passes through to the beneficiaries. There are administrative expenses of the entity that have to be paid before any residual capital gains can be passed through.

Another twist is that any net capital loss does not pass through. The Schedule D (1041) instructions on this point are very clear. They read—

*If the losses from the sale or exchange of capital assets are more than the gains, **all** of the losses must be allocated to the estate or trust and none are allocated to the beneficiaries.*

The current year net capital losses remain in the estate or trust for carryover to subsequent years. It is only when filing the "final return" of the entity that any remaining capital losses pass through.

How does a Schedule D (Form 1041) look? In most respects its Parts I for short-term and II for long-term closely resemble the corresponding Parts I and II of Schedule D (Form 1040). The noticeable difference is that there are no Schedule D-1 continuation sheets, and there are no lines for total sales price amounts. Otherwise, the applicability of indirect Forms (2439, 4684, 4797, 6252, 6781, and 8824) and a capital gain distributions line in Part II is much the same as appears on your Schedule D (Form 1040).

The major difference between a 1041 Schedule D and your 1040 Schedule D is its Part III: ***Summary of Parts I and II***. The summarizing aspect is the rearrangement of Parts I and II bottom lines into three columns, namely:

Col. (1) — *Beneficiaries'*

Col. (2) — *Estate's or trust's*
Col. (3) — *Total* [col. (1) + col. (2)]

In an abbreviated manner, we present the Part III arrangement in Figure 9.4. Not shown in Figure 9.4 is a bottom line instruction which directs—

Part III	Form 1041	Summary of Parts I and II		
FIDUCIARY DECIDES ▶		Pass to Benefic- iaries	Retain by Entity	Total Amount
Net S/T Gain/Loss				
Net L/T Gain/Loss		/////////	/////////	/////////
	a. Total for year			
	b. Unrecap.Sec.1250 gain			
	c. 28% rate gain/loss			
Total Net	¥ If Gain	**A**	**B**	**C**
Gain/Loss	¥ If Loss	/////////	< >	carry forward
	A = All, Part, or None			
	B = None, Part, or All			
	C = Grand Total			

Fig. 9.4 - Schedule D (1041) Options re Capital Gain Allocations

If a net gain . . . enter on Form 1041 [then on Schedule K-1].
If a net loss . . . [assign to the estate or trust] *then complete the* ***Capital Loss Carryover Worksheet.***

The result is that only net capital gain (short or long) passes through to beneficiaries.

Schedule K-1 (Form 1041)

The significant wording in the head portion of Schedule K-1 (1041) reads as follows:

Beneficiary's Share of Income, Deductions, Credits, etc.

▶ *Complete a separate Schedule K-1 for each beneficiary.*

Beneficiary's identifying number
Estate's or trust's EIN

And, of course, the name and address of each beneficiary, and of the fiduciary, are required.

Much unlike the K-1s of a partnership or of an S corporation, there is no requirement that the "allocable percentage" of each beneficiary be indicated. This could be a shortcoming. Fortunately, the allocable sharing aspects are (usually) clearly stated in underlying instruments: the *Last Will* for an estate; the *Trust Agreement* for a trust. Moreover, since Wills and Trusts are "family affairs," most beneficiaries know in advance what each's distributive share should be. Therefore, no real harm is done by not displaying the percentage of distributive interest for each beneficiary. To keep peace in the family, however, it is sometimes best for the fiduciary to hand enter on the K-1 the precise percentage allocable to each distributee.

There are about 40 distributive share items on a Schedule K-1 of Form 1041. Of the 40 items, only four are pertinent to our discussion in this chapter. These four are:

For current year

- *Net short-term capital* **gain**
- *Net long-term capital* **gain**

For final year

- *Short-term capital* **loss carryover**
- *Long-term capital* **loss carryover**

With the above in mind, we present in Figure 9.5 an abbreviated version of Schedule K-1 (Form 1041). Note that all distributive items are formatted into three columns. These columns are:

Col. (a) — Allocable share items
Col. (b) — Amount [in $]
Col. (c) — Where to enter on Form 1040

Sched. K-1 (Form 1041)	Beneficiary's Share of Income, etc.		Year
Beneficiary's SSN • Name & address	Estate's / Trust's EIN • Name & address		
(a) Allocable share item	**(b)** Amount	**(c)**	Where-to-enter on Form 1040
Income [No loss] • Net short-term capital gain • Net long-term capital gain	———— ————		Sched. D, Line 5, col.(f) Sched. D, line 12, col.(f)
Rents, Royalties, etc.			
Adjustments & tax preferences			
Deductions, final year • Short-term capital loss • Long-term capital loss	———— ————		Sched. D, Line 5, col.(f) Sched. D, line 12, col.(f)
Other distributions - specify			**As applicable**

Fig. 9.5 - Abbreviated Version of Schedule K-1, Form 1041

Wherever there is an amount in column (b), there is adequate adjacent white space in column (a) to hand-enter that beneficiary's distributive percentage. Such an entry is helpful for cross-checking with the Will or Trust instrument.

With respect to column (c) and the four pass-through capital items listed above, the preprinted instructions there say—

- Net short-term gain   ⟶ *Schedule D, **line 5**, col. (f)*
- Net long-term gain   ⟶ *Schedule D, **line 12**, col. (f)*
- Short-term loss carryover   ⟶ *Schedule D, **line 5**, col. (f)*
- Long-term loss carryover   ⟶ *Schedule D, **line 12**, col. (f)*

These lines 5 and 12 of Schedule D (Form 1040) are exactly the same lines onto which capital gain/loss amounts are entered from a partnership's K-1 and/or from an S corporation's K-1. This means that you should set up your own record-tracking system in the event that you are issued multiple K-1s.

Other K-1 Capital Items

In addition to the K-1 items that enter into Parts I and II of Schedule D (Form 1040), there are also several other capital items that pass through. We do not want to get into any extensive discussion of them at this time. We just want you to be aware of their existence.

One of these capital items is called: *Qualified dividends.* Maybe you've heard of them, maybe not. There is a special entry line on page 1 of Form 1040 for them. Said line (for year 2004) reads—

Line 9**b**: *Qualified dividends* $ _____

The total amount there, from K-1s and 1099-DIVs, receives special net long-term capital gain treatment. We discuss this special treatment quite extensively in Chapter 11: Qualified Dividends.

All entity K-1s (partnerships, S corporations, estates, and trusts) have a separate item/amount line captioned: Qualified dividends. The "Where to enter . . . on Form 1040" instructions state: *Form 1040, line 9b.* As you'll see in our closing chapter, the aggregate on line 9b (1040) winds up on every worksheet when following the instructions for computing the tax directly related to Schedule D (1040).

For partnerships and S corporations only, there is a Schedule K-1 amount line with is captioned: *Net section 1231 gain/<loss>.* Section 1231 of the Tax Code relates to sales and exchanges of property used in a trade or business. This is forerunner to Form 4797: *Sales of Business Property.* We addressed Form 4797 in Chapter 8: Indirect Gain/Loss Entries.

As for estates and trusts, a Form 4797 gain-only entry is provided on Schedule D (Form 1040). It is folded-in with the net long-term capital gain on Schedule D. Thus, there is no need for a separate K-1 line for this one item.

For all K-1 entities, there is one category labeled: "Net long-term capital gain." Below this entry line and amount, there is a subentry for: *Collectibles 28% rate gain.* There is also a second subentry for: *Unrecaptured section 1250 gain.* These two subitems, if applicable in your case, become computationally important when completing Part III (Summary) of your Schedule D (Form 1040). A partnership K-1, an S corporation K-1, and an estate or trust K-1, all make preprinted provisions for each of these two items. The where-to-enter instructions (on the K-1s) essentially say: See the XYZ Worksheet. If applicable, we tell you how these two subitems play out in Chapter 12: Computing Related Tax.

One final note for all Schedules K-1. The general instructions tell you to keep the K-1s for your own records. Do not attach any of them to your Form 1040 return. Each entity manager who prepares a K-1 in your name must send a copy thereof to the IRS. This one fact alone should put you on notice to follow the K-1 "where to enter on Form 1040" instructions V-E-R-Y carefully.

A Word of Caution

The whole Schedule K-1 pass-through concept originated back in 1954 with enactment of IRC Subchapter K: *Partners and Partnerships.* (Subchapter K; Schedules K and K-1: get the connection?) The initial 35-word enactment Section 701: *Partners, Not Partnership, Subject to Tax,* has not changed one iota since that time. What has changed over the years is that partnerships — and, to a lesser extent, S corporations and trusts — have become conduits for abusive tax arrangements. Included in the term "abusive" are sham transactions, artificial losses, offshore digressions, distorted valuations, nonrecourse loans, lopsided ownership interests, laundering of money, straw corporations as temporary partners, contract manipulations, and other clever schemes for underreporting the pass-through income and overreporting the pass-through deductions and credits. To curb these abuses, the **Anti-Abuse Rule** was adopted in 1994.

This particular rule is set forth in IRS Regulations 1.701-2(d): *Anti-abuse; Intent of Subchapter K.* The introductory wording to this 8,500-word regulation reads in part—

Subchapter K is intended to permit taxpayers to conduct joint business (and investment) activities through a flexible economic arrangement without incurring an entity-level tax. Included in this intent . . .are requirements that—

> *(1) The partnership be bona fide and each partnership transaction or series of related transactions be entered into for a **substantial business purpose**.*
>
> *(2) The form of each partnership transaction be viewed under **substance over form** principles.*
>
> *(3) The tax consequences to each partner . . . must accurately reflect the **partner's economic agreement** and must clearly reflect the partner's [prorata share of] income from the partnership.*

If the above principles are not readily apparent in a K-1 entity transaction, the IRS has authority to *recharacterize* that transaction [Reg. § 1.701-2(i)]. Any recharacterization is done at the entity level because that's where the brainpower for abuse focuses. Any change made by the IRS is passed through, proportionately, to each K-1 recipient.

Whether you participate, knowingly or unknowingly, in an abusive arrangement, be prepared to pay additional tax . . . plus a penalty. We must caution you in this regard should you be associated with scoundrels, who manage to hide themselves in the woodwork. Other than being the beneficiary of an estate, there are opportunists who may try to use your K-1 entity for their own tax avoidance purposes. Just don't be too naïve about the possibilities.

10

CAPITAL LOSS TREATMENT

> **For A Given Taxable Year, Capital Losses Offset Capital Gains, Dollar-For-Dollar, First Short-Term, Then Long-Term. At The End, If A Net Capital Loss Results, The Allowable Loss For That Year Is THE LOWEST OF: (1) $3,000; (2) The Net Loss Itself; Or (3) Your Adjusted Taxable Income. Any Excess Is Carried Forward to Subsequent Years To Offset Capital Gains In Those Years. In Two Specific Cases, Sales Of Business Property (Sec. 1231) And Small Business Stock (Sec. 1244), Capital Losses Are DEEMED TO BE Ordinary Losses And Are Not Subject To The Capital Loss Limitation Of $3,000 Per Year.**

The primary focus of Schedule D (1040) is on net capital gain. If an amount of the net is long-term, preferential tax rates apply. If an amount is short-term, ordinary tax rates apply. Either way, the gain is recognized and taxed in full in the year of its occurrence.

But, what if there is a net capital loss instead? Is it recognized and allowed in full?

The short answer is "Yes" IF . . . the net loss is $3,000 or less in the occurrence year. If the net loss exceeds $3,000, the excess can be carried forward and consumed at the rate of $3,000 per year thereafter.

For example, suppose you incurred a $30,000 *net* capital loss (short-term or long-term: not much difference). If you had no capital gains in the loss occurrence year or in subsequent years, it would take 10 years to consume the capital loss!

What is the rationale for the $3,000 per year limitation with net capital losses?

There is really no acceptable rationale. The only explanation that we've been able to find is that: "It's a political tradeoff." Because the opponents to preferential capital gain rates "had to give a little," the proponents for allowing full capital losses also had to give a little. Politically, it is always more popular to extol the virtues of capital gains. Any hint of the possibility of capital losses is negative. It is bad for morale, business, and the national economy. The political "spin machines" all like gains.

In this chapter, however, we *have to* address the possibility of capital losses. Primarily because Schedule D (1040) uses and preprints the word "loss" almost as frequently — but not quite — as the word "gain." In addressing capital losses, we also have to distinguish between personal transactional losses (from personal use property) and operational transactional losses (from business use property). Personal losses are not tax recognized. Business property losses are treated as ordinary (operational) losses. This means that said losses bypass entirely the $3,000 per year capital loss limitation rule.

Persons who qualify as "investors" (as per Chapter 2 earlier) always have to wrestle with capital loss situations. For your wrestling match, we present in this chapter some very useful knowledge and guidelines. After all, capital losses do have some positive side effects.

"The Law" on Point

The specific tax law which addresses capital losses is Section 1211. Its official heading is: *Limitation on Capital Losses*. Subsection (b) thereof is titled: *Other Taxpayers*. This means individuals and others than a corporation.

Section 1211(b) specifically addresses the subject of net capital losses for individuals. The entire section reads—

*In the case of a taxpayer other than a corporation, losses from sales or exchanges of capital assets shall be allowed only to the extent of the gains from such sales or exchanges, plus (if such losses exceed such gains) the **lower** of—*

(1) $3,000 ($1,500 in the case of a married individual filing a separate return), or
(2) the excess of such losses over such gains.

The statute seems pretty clear: $3,000 net loss limit (period). If married, you can't increase this limit to $6,000 by filing separate returns. By statute, each spouse filing separately is limited to $1,500 in net capital loss. This $1,500 married-separate limitation is often overlooked during the haste of preparation at tax time.

On Schedule D (1040), Part III: **Summary**, the capital loss limitation rule shows up as follows:

Step 1 — *Combine lines _____ and _____, and enter the result. If a loss, go to line _____ [Step 2].*

Step 2 — *If [Step 1] is a loss, enter here [in < >] and on Form 1040, line _____ [on page 1], the **smaller** of:*
• The loss on line _____ [Step 1], or
• <3,000> or, if married filing separately, <1,500>.

What is the essence of the above?

It is that if your net capital loss for the year is $3,000 or less (for single, head of household, or married filing jointly), you can use up to that amount to offset other sources of income on Form 1040. Altogether, there are 15 other sources of income on page 1 of Form 1040. By combining with "other sources," a capital loss can help reduce your total income on page 1.

What we are talking about here are **net** capital losses (for a given year). That is, after all Schedule D gains, if any, have been taken into account. For netting purposes in a given year, distinctions between short-term and long-term are not significant. Capital losses offset capital gains, dollar-for-dollar, until a net/net bottom line capital loss results.

Within a given year, if there are any capital gains, the tax-recognized capital losses may be the amount of those capital gains *plus* $3,000. For example, suppose you have $25,000 in capital gains for the year. If applicable, you could write off on Schedule D as much as $28,000 in capital losses. The net/net would be $3,000 loss to write off against non-Schedule D sources of income.

Thus, there is some positive benefit even with a current year net loss limitation.

If More Than $3,000 Loss

Suppose your net capital loss for the year is more than $3,000. Do you lose the excess loss over $3,000?

No; you do not.

There is a carryforward feature which allows you to write off the unused capital loss in future years. The carryforward feature goes on indefinitely . . . or until you die. If you are married (filing jointly), and your spouse dies, you can still carry forward the unused loss until you die. At that point, any still unused capital loss carryforward becomes a "loss/loss." It cannot be picked up and deducted on your death tax (estate) return.

The amount of capital loss carryforward *each year* is limited to $3,000 plus any offsetting capital gains. It is a repetitive process: $3,000 net loss write-off each year, until the total net capital loss (for the computational year) is used up.

The tax law on point is Section 1212(b): *Capital Loss Carrybacks and Carryovers; Other Taxpayers*. This section is substantially more complex than the $3,000 loss limitation section above. So, we'll present the carryforward feature first. Carryforwards (carryovers) are far more applicable to ordinary investors than carrybacks.

Section 1212(b)(1) reads in significant part as follows:

If a taxpayer other than a corporation has a net capital loss for any taxable year—
   (A) the excess of the net short-term capital loss over the net long-term capital gain for such year shall be a short-term capital loss in the succeeding taxable year, and
   (B) the excess of the net long-term capital loss over the net short-term capital gain for such year shall be a long-term capital loss in the succeeding taxable year.

In other words, if you have a net capital loss in excess of $3,000 for a given year, you have to go back over your Schedule D, and determine which portion of the excess loss is short-term and which is long-term. The short-term carryover losses are subsequent-year consumed first.

If "Negative" Taxable Income

The carryover/carryforward rules above are based on the assumption that the taxpayer has positive taxable income, irrespective of his $3,000 loss from Schedule D. If he has other losses (current-year plus prior-year carryovers, if any) that do not appear on Schedule D, the taxpayer/investor — it could be you — might have *negative* taxable income. If this is the case, the amount of capital loss carryforward becomes a notch more complex.

The rule on point is Section 1212(b)(2): **Treatment of Amounts Allowed Under Section 1211(b)(1) or (2).** We refrain from quoting this statute because it will only confuse you. It says, in essence, that if one has a negative taxable income, one cannot drive the negative amount more negative by including a $3,000 capital loss. By definition, taxable income cannot go below zero. When there is zero taxable income, there is zero tax. End of computation for that taxable year. Section 1212(b)(2) recognizes this reality by introducing the computational reference: *adjusted taxable income.*

The term "adjusted taxable income" is simply your regular taxable income BEFORE any deductions for personal exemptions. In other words, you compute your adjusted gross income as you would ordinarily (using Schedule D). Then deduct your itemized deductions or standard deduction, as appropriate. If the result is a positive amount more than $3,000, steam ahead. If the positive amount is less than $3,000, the capital loss allowable for the year becomes **the least of—**

(1) $3,000 or, if married filing separately, $1,500;
(2) excess of losses over gains on Schedule D; or
(3) adjusted taxable income.

If the adjusted taxable income itself is negative, no capital loss is allowed for that year.

The idea underlying Section 1212(b)(2) is to give you a slight break. It increases your capital loss carryforward when you have an adjusted taxable income of less than $3,000. Anything less than $3,000 increases the recognized carryforward correspondingly. For example, if your adjusted taxable income is $1,000, you consume only $1,000 of the $3,000 loss limit. This increases your loss carryforward by an additional $2,000.

Capital Loss Carryovers

How do you compute and record your capital loss carryover for the current year . . . and for each successive carryforward year (when applicable)? Strangely, the computation does not appear on Schedule D itself. So, where does it appear? To find out, let's go back to Schedule D (1040) and see what it says about capital loss carryovers. Part III of Schedule D is titled: *Summary*. After telling you to use the smallest of $3,000 etc., it says—

Next: Complete Form 1040 through line _____ [adjusted taxable income]. *Then, complete the **Capital Loss Carryover Worksheet** on page* _____ [of the Schedule D instructions].

You'll have to dig up this Worksheet on your own. It is not preprinted directly on Schedule D.

This raises the question: "Why isn't the capital loss carryover computation a preprinted part of Schedule D?" Think about this for a moment.

Would we be cynical to suggest that Congress, the financial markets, and the IRS prefer that you forget about your loss carryovers? None of these sources wants to focus on your losses. Mentioning losses is bad politics; it damages marketing hype; and it deprives the IRS of revenue. It requires hard work and effort to compute, track, and claim your loss carryforwards. Nobody likes hard work. Especially when the loss carryforward worksheet requires reexamination of the prior year's capital losses

We've gone to the trouble of digging up the Worksheet from the instructions for you. Its headnote instruction says—

Keep for your records. . . . Capital losses that exceed your amount of capital gains plus $3,000 ($1,500 if married filing separately), are carried forward to later years.

How do you carry forward to later years? First, you have to locate and complete the Worksheet. Then you set it aside for a year. The year following the year of occurrence of the net capital loss, you look for two specific lines on the front page of Schedule D. One line is in Part I (short-term); the other line is in Part II (long-term). Recall that "short-term" pertains to assets held one year or less; "long-term" when held more than one year.

Part I loss carryforward line **6** (2004 version) reads:

Short-term capital loss carryover. Enter the amount, if any, from line _____ of your [prior year] *Capital Loss Carryover Worksheet.*

Correspondingly, Part II line **14** (2004 version) reads:

Long-term capital loss carryover. Enter the amount, if any, from line _____ of your [prior year] *Capital Loss Carryover Worksheet.*

The general idea behind the Capital Loss Carryover Worksheet is to separate your *prior year's* net capital loss into two "baskets." One basket is for short-term losses (as in Part I above), and the other is for long-term losses (as in Part II above). Short-term (prior year) losses are first carried over to offset your current year's short-term capital gains, if any. Similarly, long-term (prior year) losses are carried over to offset your current year's long-term capital gains, if any. To prepare the Worksheet, you must retrieve your prior year's tax return: Form 1040 and its Schedule D. You need to do this, even if you have a computer software program that will do the Worksheet for you.

For both the Part I and Part II Schedule D baskets, each loss carryover amount is entered into column (f): **Gain or <loss>**. There it combines with all other gains and losses in that column. The loss carryover, if any, is the last entry in each part of Schedule D before subtotaling that part. The gist of what we are getting at here is portrayed in Figure 10.1. Note that the Parts I and II loss "netting" is established in Part III.

If you have no prior year net capital loss carryovers, the IRS-prepared worksheet is not required.

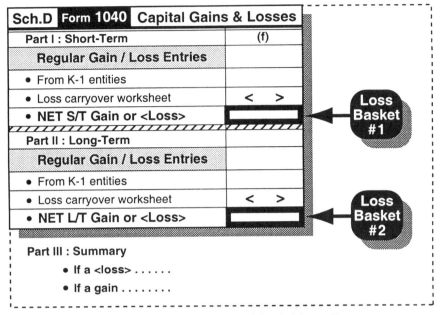

Fig. 10.1 - Rate Basket Prioritizing of Capital Loss Carryovers

Worksheet Rule of Thumb

The Capital Loss Carryover Worksheet for your Schedule D consists of 13 computational lines. We are tempted to step through each of the 13 lines with you, but we don't think you'd read them. They are tedious and confusing. They involve many Form 1040 and Schedule D prior year cross-line referencing. Even with a computer software Worksheet, we think you'd skip over scrolling down line by line. Why do you think the IRS calls it a "WORKsheet"? We have a simpler way.

Our way is called "rule of thumb and common sense." At this point, let us assume that you have no prior year capital loss carryovers. That is, your current year is your first net capital loss year. With this assumption in mind, our way goes like this:

Rule of Thumb: Combine the net capital losses in Parts I and II of your current return. Treat the combination as *all* short-term. Subtract the current year's allowable loss. Then treat all of the excess as your capital loss carryover to next year. Make a hand notation to this effect in the ample white space below Part III of Schedule D. For your carryover year, make an "eyeball" allocation between the Parts I and II carryovers, keeping in mind that the short-term residuals are consumed first on your next year's return. The IRS does NOT computer match your loss carryovers, the way it does with the gross proceeds from your sales and those sales reported by your broker. Even in a loss sale, the "gross proceeds" are a positive amount.

For example, suppose your net capital loss for the current year is $21,000. After subtracting your current year's allowable $3,000 loss (married filing jointly), your residual loss for carryforward purposes would be $18,000. If your Part I (short-term) net loss were $10,000, say, your Part I carryover loss would be $7,000 (10,000 – 3,000). Correspondingly, your Part II (long-term) carryover loss to next year would be $11,000 (18,000 – 7,000).

Make your loss carryover notation as we indicate in Figure 10.2. Do this by hand on your own copy of the Schedule D, even though you may have a software program that does the Worksheet for you. This way, you'll be self-reminded next year that you have a capital loss carryover to be used. Whether it is short-term or long-term, your carryforward is a useable loss.

Carryback of Certain Losses

We are not through with Section 1212 yet: Capital Loss Carrybacks and Carryovers. Above, we've covered the loss carryover part only. Now, let's look at the carry**back** part. When we do, an unusual rule applies.

The unusual loss carryback rule is Section 1212(**c**): *Carryback of Losses from Section 1256 Contracts to Offset Prior Gains from Such Contracts*. A "Section 1256 contract" is any regulated futures contract, foreign currency contract, nonequity (nonownership) option, or dealer equity option. The applicable tax form is **Form 6781**: *Gains and Losses from Contracts and Straddles*. This is one of the seven associated-with-Schedule D forms that we covered in Chapter 8. These marked-to-market contracts (on the last business day of the year) are the domain for go-go investors.

Part III	SUMMARY	Capital Gains & Losses	Sch. D

A
Combine lines ___ and ___ [in Parts I and II]
IF a **loss**, enter here,
and go to line ___ below.   _____

> **LOSS CARRYOVER**
> **REMINDER** < $ >

B
Enter **SMALLER** of these losses:
• <$3,000> or <$1,500> MFS
• Net capital loss above   _____
• Adjusted taxable income
  Enter on page 1, Form 1040

Subtract **B** from **A** . This is your combined capital loss carryover. >

Fig. 10.2 - Entering Loss Carryover Reminder in Part III of Schedule D

Section 1212(c) consists of approximately 700 words. The gist is that you may carry back your capital losses—

To each of the 3 taxable years preceding the loss year, and to the extent that . . . such loss is allowed as a carryback . . .
(i)   40 percent . . . shall be treated as a short-term capital loss . . . and,
(ii)   60 percent . . . shall be treated as a long-term capital loss . . . [separately for each carryback year].

Other portions of Section 1212(c) tell you that you must "coordinate" your carryback losses with the $3,000 per year computational limit on net capital losses from all associated forms. In other words, you cannot use Section 1256 carryback losses to exceed the $3,000 loss limitation described above.

The 3-year carryback rule for Section 1256 losses is *elective*; it is not mandatory. The election is signified by checking a box on Form 6781 that reads—

☐ *Net section 1256 contracts loss election*

If you elect the carryback provision, you go back three tax years on Schedule D and start working forward. If you do this, subsection 1212(c)(3) tells you that you can only use the carryback losses to offset Section 1256 gains (if any) that previously occurred in the carryback years. You cannot use Section 1256 carryback losses to offset non-section 1256 gains.

There is a very special reason why you are allowed to carry back losses on contracts and straddles. In the carryback years, before the loss carrybacks, you were forced to "mark-to-market" your unrealized gains (on unexpired positions) at the end of each year. If you reported Section 1256 unrealized gains for the carryback years, you are entitled to reduce them for subsequent-year realized losses. You are not allowed this carryback feature for any other capital transactions as an individual.

Section 1231 Loss Conversion

Back in Chapters 8 and 9, we introduced you to Section 1231 in conjunction with **Form 4797**: *Sales of Business Property*. We pointed out then that Section 1231 is known as the capital gain/ordinary loss rule. It applies strictly only to property used in a trade or business, or for income production, when held more than one year. Form 4797 is so structured that if a series of sales and exchanges results in a net long-term capital loss, the preprinted instructions direct its conversion into an *ordinary* loss. We pictorialized this conversion process in Figure 8.2 (on page 8-10). Now we want to explain the conversion more fully.

As you may recall, Section 1231 is titled: **Property Used in the Trade or Business and Involuntary Conversions**. The portion pertinent here is subsection 1231(a)(2). It reads—

> *If the section 1231 gains, for any taxable year, do not exceed the section 1231 losses for such taxable year, such gains and losses **shall not** be treated as gains and losses from sales or exchanges of capital assets.* [Emphasis added.]

In plain language, this wording says that if there are net Section 1231 losses, they are not to be treated as capital losses. Then how are such losses to be treated?

You have to read subsection 1231(a)(4) to find out. Said subsection reads—

The section 1231 losses shall be included only if and to the extent taken into account in computing taxable income, except that section 1211 shall not apply.

Section 1211, recall, is: Limitation on Capital Losses . . . at $3,000 per year. The wording "taken into account in computing taxable income" means that the net 1231 loss **bypasses** Schedule D and goes — via Form 4797, Part II (Ordinary Gains and Losses) — directly onto Form 1040. Once on Form 1040, the losses combine with other income and losses to establish one's total income.

A schematization of how the net Section 1231 losses (noncapital) combine to produce total income is presented in Figure 10.3. Note that we show the Schedule D loss limitation of $3,000. Ordinary losses have no such limitation. That is why we show in Figure 10.3 the loss amount in < > as "open."

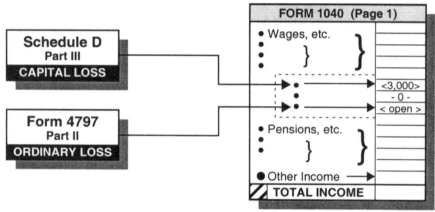

Fig. 10.3 - How Sch. D and Form 4797 Losses Appear on Form 1040

The only limitation to ordinary losses is a practical one. Since said losses combine directly with all non-Schedule D sources of income, the limitation is — should said losses be so great — the driving of one's total income negative. To the extent that the total income goes below zero, one has a net operating loss (NOL) for that year. Should this happen, an entirely different loss carryback/

carryover rule comes into play, namely: Section 172(b): Net Operating Loss (NOL) Deduction. An NOL must derive strictly from a trade or business regardless of the form of business.

There is still one other Section 1231 feature that we haven't told you about. It is subsection (**c**): *Recapture of Net Ordinary Loss*. This is a "reverse conversion" rule. The essence is that, after incurring a net capital loss for a given year which was converted to an ordinary loss, any net capital gain in the next subsequent five years is reverse converted to ordinary income. There is a separate entry line in Part I of Form 4797 for this purpose. The extent of the recapture conversion is limited to the amount of prior ordinary loss converted from capital loss. In other words, if the amount of capital loss converted to ordinary loss was $24,635, say, the amount of subsequent capital gain reverse converted to ordinary income would not exceed $24,635. This is one of those "payback" quirks that often appear in tax laws.

Section 1244 Stock Losses

There are still other kinds of investment losses that are treated as ordinary (noncapital) losses. Foremost in this regard are Section 1244 losses. Section 1244 is titled: *Losses on Small Business Stock*. Similar treatment is given to Section 1242 (Losses on small business investment company stock) and to Section 1243 (Loss of small business investment company).

A "small business corporation" is a trade or business entity whose total stock authorized and issued does not exceed $1,000,000 (1 million). To qualify for ordinary loss treatment, the corporation must issue specifically designated *Section 1244 stock.* Such stock must be issued for money or in exchange for readily marketable property. Issuance in exchange for other stock or securities does not qualify. The term "1244 stock" is a tax character designation: not a class of ownership. The tax-recognized losses on such stock cannot exceed $100,000 for married investors filing jointly, and $50,000 for single persons (or married filing separately). This is the maximum loss tax allowed for any given taxable year.

The citations on point are Sections 1244(a) and 1244(b). These sections, in pertinent part, read as follows:

(a) In the case of an individual, a loss on section 1244 stock issued to such individual or to a partnership which would (but for this section) be treated as a loss from the sale or exchange of a capital asset shall, to the extent provided [herein], *be treated as an **ordinary loss**.*

(b) For any taxable year the aggregate amount treated . . . as an ordinary loss shall not exceed—

(1) $50,000 or

(2) $100,000 in the case of a husband and wife filing a joint return for such year. [Emphasis added.]

In a Section 1244 loss situation, how would the ordinary loss be signified on your tax return?

It would *not* go on Schedule D. It goes on Form 4797, Part II (Ordinary Gains and Losses). Do not confuse Part II of Form 4797 with Part II of Schedule D.

Part II of Form 4797 consists of several direct entry lines, each segmented into seven columns (a) through (g), as shown in Figure 10.4. These columns are analogous to those on Schedule D, except column (e). This column is captioned: *Depreciation allowed or allowable since acquisition.* An allowance for depreciation is indicative of business property transactions for which Form 4797 is designed (and for which recapture rules apply). Column (f) is *Cost or other basis*; column (g) is *Gain or <loss> for entire year.*

If you have a loss from Section 1244 stock, you enter in column (a) the description: "Sec. 1244 stock." You then fill in the other applicable columns (enter -0- in column (e)) ending with a loss amount in column (g). You proceed down the form to the instruction which directs you to page 1 of Form 1040. There, the ordinary loss amount offsets your other ordinary income without concern for the $3,000 capital loss limitation.

Bad Debt: Business v. Nonbusiness

One of the most difficult loss concepts to understand is the tax treatment of bad debts. A "bad debt" is the advancement of money, property, or services for which a bona fide obligation to pay back is created. That is, a true arm's-length creditor-debtor relationship exists. Repeated efforts to collect on the debt have been made . . . to no avail. It becomes a total loss. The situation is unlike that of acquiring stock, bonds, or other securities which become worthless. How do you claim a bad debt loss on your tax return? Do you claim it on Schedule D as a capital loss? Or, do you claim it elsewhere as an ordinary loss?

Part II	Form 4797	SALES OF BUSINESS PROPERTY				
ORDINARY GAINS & LOSSES (Including items held 1 year or less)						
(a)	(b)	(c)	(d)	(e)	(f)	(g)
Descrip-tion	Date Acq.	Date Sold	Sales Price	Depr. Allowed	Cost Basis	Gain or <Loss>
• Loss, if any, from line ____ [Part I]						< >
• Gain, if any, from line ____ [Part I]						
• Gain, if any, from line ____ [Part III]						
• Gain/loss from associated forms						
/////	NET ORDINARY GAIN OR <LOSS> • Enter here & on Form 1040, page 1					

Fig. 10.4 - Contents: Part II of Form 4797: For Ordinary Losses

The answer is: It all depends. It depends on the nature and purpose of the debt when it was initially created. If its purpose was primarily trade or business oriented, its worthlessness becomes an ordinary loss. If its purpose was primarily investment oriented, its worthlessness becomes a capital loss on Schedule D. If the debt — no matter what the pretense — is between family members and close business associates, it is tax treated as a personal loss. As such, neither Schedule D nor any other schedule can be used.

The tax law on point is Section 166: **Bad Debts.** Its subsection (a)(1): **Wholly Worthless Debts,** says—

There shall be allowed as a deduction any debt which becomes worthless within the taxable year.

In addition, subsection (b): *Amount of Deduction*, says—

The basis for determining the amount of the deduction for any bad debt shall be the adjusted basis . . . for determining the loss from the sale or other disposition of property.

There are two types of bad debts: business and nonbusiness. Given a choice, you'd like the bad debt to be "business" rather than nonbusiness. A *business bad debt* is defined as—

A debt created or acquired (as the case may be) in connection with a trade or business of the taxpayer; or a debt the loss from the worthlessness of which is incurred in the taxpayer's trade or business. [Sec. 166(d)(2)(A) and (B)].

The key here is what constitutes a "trade or business." It is the day-to-day participation in an ongoing effort to attract customers and clients, in order to sell them products or render them services. The creditor-debtor relationship must have arisen as a direct consequence of these activities. The debt must be ordinary and necessary as a customary mode of operation, or it must be a dominant concern in seeking to improve operations. If it can be demonstrated that these conditions indeed exist, the amount uncollectible is a *business* bad debt. It is thereby deductible in full, without limitation. The loss claim is made on one of the following: Schedule C (1040): *Profit or Loss from Business*; Schedule F (1040): *Profit or Loss from Farming*; Form 1065: *Partnership Return of Income*; Form 1120: *Corporation Income Tax Return*; Form 1120S: *Income Tax Return for an S Corporation*; or Form 4797, Part II: *Sales of Business Property, Ordinary Losses*. An estate or trust is NOT a trade or business. Nor is investing.

It has long been held that full-time engagement with one's investments, no matter how extensive, does not constitute a trade or business. [*E. Higgins*, SCt, 41-1 USTC ¶ 9233.] Also, in *A. J. Whipple*, SCt, 63-1 USTC ¶ 9466, the Court said:

When the only return [profit or gain] *is that of an investor, the taxpayer has not satisfied his burden of demonstrating that he* *is engaged in a trade or business since **investing is not a trade or business**.* [Emphasis added.]

Unless a creditor can clearly demonstrate that a trade or business dominance is involved, any purported bad debt is tax deemed to be a *nonbusiness* bad debt. As such, and pursuant to Section 166(d)(1)(A) and (B), the uncollectible amount is treated as a **short-term capital loss**. This means making a direct entry in Part I of Schedule D, where it combines with other direct entries.

Undercapitalization Losses

The term "undercapitalization" applies where a taxpayer (investor/entrepreneur) forms his own corporation, then tries to bootstrap his operation with minimum contributions of capital. Pretty soon, the corporate entity needs more money. The incorporator borrows money from a financial institution which requires his personal guarantee and personal assets as collateral. The business fails; the taxpayer's guarantee is called. Is the resulting loss an ordinary (business) loss? Or, is it a capital (nonbusiness) loss? The answer is different from what you might reasonably think.

To give you the "flavor" of the answers that emerge, we cite three different court rulings on the same issue.

The case of *D.L. Atkinson*, 48 TCM 577, TC Memo. 1984-378, involved the personal guarantee on two bank loans (totaling $74,892) taken out by Atkinson's own corporation. The corporation was able to pay back $51,904 before it ceased business. Atkinson made good on the unrepaid $22,988 from his own funds. Subsequently, he claimed an ordinary loss for the $22,988. The IRS said "No; it was a capital loss." The Court sided with the IRS. It reasoned that because the corporation was unable to pay the money, Atkinson's $22,988 was a *contribution of capital* to his undercapitalized company. As such, he was entitled to short-term capital loss treatment only.

In *G. Peterson*, 74 TCM 335, TC Memo. 1997-377, the taxpayer acted as a guarantor of his corporation's $350,000 line of credit. The corporation failed, whereupon the bank foreclosed on Peterson's home to satisfy the unpaid debt. Peterson claimed the foreclosure as an ordinary loss. This produced an NOL with its 3-year loss carryback provisions. The IRS disallowed this treatment entirely. The Court concurred by ruling that—

> The payments made on the guarantee represented contributions to the capital of the company's undercapitalized line of credit, not loans, and gave rise to a capital loss, subject to the limitations of Code Sec. 1211.

In *C.E. Pierce*, BC-DC Okla, 94-2 USTC ¶ 50,627, the taxpayer, a real estate developer, was an 85% owner and president of a small commercial bank. He contributed $595,000 to the bank entity in exchange for his shares of stock. Still, the bank was having financial difficulties. Thereupon, Pierce loaned the bank $325,868 from his own funds, "to keep the bank afloat." When the bank went bankrupt, Pierce claimed the $325,868 as a business bad debt (ordinary loss). The Court denied this treatment by ruling that—

> The evidence reveals that Pierce's dominant motivation in making the loan was to protect his substantial investment in the bank. Therefore, Pierce's claimed bad debt deduction of $325,868 under IRS Sec. 166 . . . is disallowed. However, the Court finds Pierce's $325,868 loss to be a capital loss for the taxable year, deductible to the extent, if any, allowed by IRC Sec. 1211(b).

As you can sense from most of the above, it is very difficult to circumvent the $3,000 per year capital loss limitation rule. If you are an investor, Section 1211(b) is something you'll just have to learn to live with.

11

QUALIFIED DIVIDENDS

When Dividends Are Paid To Shareholders From The Earnings And Profits Of A Public Corporation, The Term "Qualified" Means Qualified For Capital Gain Treatment. The Treatment Is Long-Term Capital Gain Even Though The Holding Period Is Short-Term: 61 Days In A 121-Day Consecutive Period (Beginning 60 Days Before The Ex-Dividend Date). This Means Your Getting The Benefit Of Significantly Reduced Tax Rates - Either 5% Or 15% - Compared To Ordinary Rates Of 10% Through 35%. To Receive This Favorable Treatment, A Comprehensive (19-Line) Qualified Dividends Tax Worksheet Has To Be Traversed. It Can Be Shortened In Some Cases.

There's a new kid on the block for Schedule D treatment. The activity is called: Qualified dividends. The term "dividends," as you already know, applies to the distribution to shareholders of a corporation some or all of its earnings and profits. The term "qualified" means that certain dividends participate in the favorable (lower) tax rates of long-term capital gains. Year 2003 was the first time that qualified dividends appeared on the scene.

Qualified dividends have three characteristics that distinguish them from traditional long-term capital gains. One distinction is the holding period requirement. There is a 61-day holding period for qualifying "ordinary" dividends, and, separately, a 91-day holding period for qualifying "preferred" dividends. Both holding periods are referenced to the corporation's ex-dividend date (which we'll explain later).

The second distinction is that nowhere in Part II (long-term) of Schedule D does the term: "qualified dividends" appear. The term is mentioned in **Part III**: *Summary*, by a direct question at line 22: *Do you have qualified dividends?* ☐ *Yes*, ☐ *No*. Line 22 is the last computational instruction on Schedule D for year 2004.

The third distinction is that qualified dividends are set to sunset — expire — after December 31, 2008. Unless the applicable legislation is amended, the now popular 15% capital gains rate reverts to the year 2002 rate of 20%. As of this writing (in 2005), it is not clear that the concept of qualified dividends will continue beyond 2008.

Accordingly, in this chapter we want to explain the rationale behind the legislatively-created concept of qualified dividends, how such dividends are claimed on Form 1040 and on Schedule D, how they are reported to the IRS by corporate declarants, and, finally, how the *Qualified Dividends and Capital Gain Tax Worksheet* works in your favor. Our belief is that as investors become accustomed to the "softening" of the double-taxation aspect of corporate dividends via qualified dividends, the sunset provisions could be altered or repealed.

Leadoff Statutory Wording

Section 1 of the Internal Revenue Code is a mandatory embodiment by Congress. Its official title is: *Tax Imposed [on Individuals]*. It consists of approximately 7,000 statutory words. Quite far down in this embodiment is a subsection captioned: *Dividends taxed as net capital gains* [subsec. 1(h)(11)]. This caption alone gives you a hint that qualified dividends are taxed as capital gains (long term). They are not taxed as ordinary income, as has been the case traditionally. Thus, something new, indeed, has been added to our repertoire of capital gains and losses.

Paragraph (A) of subsection 1(h)(11): *In general*, states that—

For purposes of this subsection, the term "net capital gain" means net capital gain (determined without regard to this paragraph) **increased** *by qualified dividend income.* [Emphasis added.]

This wording is cryptic in style. One has to know beforehand what net capital gain means . . . "without regard to" qualified dividends. Traditionally, the term net capital gain has always meant the netting of all capital gains and losses in Part I of Schedule D (short-term) with those in Part II (long-term) thereof. If the net/net result is long-term capital gain, you have what is called: "net capital gain." Cryptically, then, you have to complete Parts I and II of Schedule D before you go to Part III. It is in Part III: *Summary* where you increase the net capital gain by qualified dividend income. This is why the term "qualified dividends" does not appear in either Part I or Part II of Schedule D.

What happens if there is no net capital gain? That is, you have a net capital loss (be it short- or long-term). what happens then?

Answer: You still get net capital gain treatment for your qualified dividends. The statutory wording does not say this, but the procedural wording in Part III of Schedule D does. You are asked: *Do you have qualified dividends?* ☐ *Yes* ☐ *No.* If you answer "Yes," you are instructed to complete the *Qualified Dividends and Capital Gain Tax Worksheet*. If you have no net capital gain or no capital gain distributions, you simply enter zero on the indicated worksheet line, and proceed onward. The point is that, even with a net capital loss from Parts I and II, you do not lose favorable tax treatment for qualified dividends. This is a new special benefit which truly is untraditional.

The Rationale of Congress

It is appropriate now to review what Congress had in mind when it enacted the qualified dividends rule [subsec. 1(h)(11)(A)]. This provision was enacted on May 28, 2003 as just one part of a much broader public law, namely: the Jobs and Growth Tax Relief Reconciliation Act (JGTRRA). With respect to dividends distributed by corporations to their shareholders, the "tax relief" was in the form of a tax rate reduction. By recharacterizing certain dividends as capital gains, individual rates could be reduced from a high of 35% to a norm of 15%. Such was the objective of the JGTRRA Joint Senate/House Committee of Congress.

In a section headed: *Dividend income — Reason for Change*, the Committee report on JGTRRA states in part that—

> *The Committee believes that reducing the individual tax on dividends lowers the cost of capital and will lead to economic growth and the creation of jobs. . . . In addition, reducing the aggregate tax burden on investments made by corporations will lower the cost of capital needed to finance new investments and lead to increases in private sector employment. It is through such investment that the United States economy can increase output, employment, and productivity that workers earn higher real wages and all Americans benefit from a higher standard of living.*

So much for published "legislative spin"!

In practice, a quite different corporate financing situation was happening. Instead of successful corporations passing through their earnings and profits to their shareholders — for which they got no tax deductions — the corporate elite used the shareholders' money for other purposes. Their "other purposes" provided corporate tax deductions in the form of: (a) stratospheric salaries and bonuses to CEOs and their staff; (b) paying interest on multi-million/mega-billion debt instruments (instead of issuing new equity stock); (c) buying stock in other dividend-paying corporations (for which there was a dividends-received deduction of 70% to 100%); and (d) transferring undistributed earnings and profits to offshore tax havens where no further U.S. tax need be paid. These offshore havens, especially when camouflaged as subsidiary foreign partnerships, lead to egregious tax avoidance schemes by the corporate elite. The resulting greed and fraud deprive ordinary shareholders of their rightful benefits.

The JGTRRA Committee reports do not delve into these other-purpose uses of shareholder money. Nevertheless, some outspoken members of Congress have done so. They have tactfully dubbed such corporate malfeasance as the deliberate distortion of capital markets. Easing this distortion is probably the fundamental reason for enactment of subsection 1(h)(11)(A).

More on Meaning of "Qualified"

Paragraph (B) of subsection 1(h)(11) is captioned: *Qualified dividend income*. Subparagraph (i) thereof states that—

The term "qualified dividend income" means dividends received during the taxable year from . . . domestic corporations and qualified foreign corporations.

Without this statutory wording actually saying so, the term "corporation" (whether domestic or foreign) applies only to a *public* corporation. A public corporation is one whose shares can be bought, sold, and freely traded on established securities markets in the U.S. Public corporations pay dividends to their shareholder, more or less regularly. The dividends are paid from the earnings and profits of the entrepreneurial business operations of the shareholder entity.

The presumption is that the shareholders in a public corporation "own" the earnings and profits of the entity in which they risk their contributory capital. This "public" feature rules out dividends, if any, from corporations that are private, charitable, government, or special purpose. The IRS lists some 12 corporate-type entities whose dividends do not qualify for capital gain treatment. Special rules apply when dividends are paid to employees, creditors, lenders, and to other corporations. While these dividend recipients technically may be shareholders, they are not members of the investing general public for which the qualified dividend concept was intended. The concept primarily is to reward ordinary shareholders who risk their investment capital.

Qualified foreign corporations are those which are:

(a) incorporated in a possession of the U.S.,
(b) registered on an established securities market in the U.S., or
(c) incorporated in a country which is a party to a comprehensive income tax treaty with the U.S. Currently, about 45 countries have been tax treaty confirmed.

So long as the dividend income emanates from a qualified corporation, some or all of said dividends may qualify for capital gain treatment. Those that do qualify for capital gain treatment are called: "qualified dividends"; those that do not qualify are called: "ordinary dividends." Both types may be paid to shareholders directly, or indirectly through mutual funds, partnerships, S corporations, estates, and/or trusts.

A source of terminology confusion exists when reporting dividends to shareholders. The gross amount of dividends — qualified **and** nonqualified — are reported to the IRS officially as: *Total ordinary dividends.* From this total, the recipient subtracts the qualified dividends to separate out the ordinary dividends. You do this through prescribed computational procedures, rather than simply making the subtraction in your head. There is a default reason for this. If you do not follow the official worksheet procedures on Schedule D, you default into paying ordinary tax rates on qualified dividends.

Holding Period Requirements

The holding period of stock for qualified dividend treatment is referenced to an *ex-dividend* date. The "dividend date" is that date on which the declaring corporation finalizes its list of shareholders who are to receive dividends. The list includes not only the name of each shareholder, his/her number of shares held, but also his/her Tax ID number. The listing eventually goes to the IRS for dividend income report-matching. The dividend date is usually made known to shareholders 30 days or so before its finalization. The "ex-dividend" date is one day *after* the dividend date is established.

The ex-dividend date is strictly a discretionary option of the corporation itself. Individual shareholders have no influence on the selection of such date. Usually, however, the date is set to coincide with, or near, the end of each calendar quarter: March 31, June 30, September 30, and December 31. If such calendar-quarter-end occurs on a Monday, the ex-dividend date is often set to occur on the last stock-trading day of that month. This is for paperwork convenience . . . especially for the month of December. Most individual shareholders are calendar-year filers of their income tax returns.

There is a 61-day holding period rule for qualified dividends paid on common stock. That is, the shareholder must hold his stock for more than 61 days in a consecutive period of 121 days. The 121 days must include the ex-dividend date. For example, suppose the ex-dividend date was March 31. If the shareholder acquired his stock on March 1, he would have held the stock for just 30 days on March 31. (The date of acquisition does *not* count as a holding day.) If he sold the stock on April 30 (the day of sale or other disposition counts as a holding day), he would have held the stock for only 60 days. The qualifying rule calls for *more than* 61 days. So the sale, if any, would have to be made on May 2 . . . or later (but no later than May 31).

The 121-day eligibility period starts 60 days before the ex-dividend date, and ends 61 days after said date. Somewhere in this spread period, a total of more than 61 days must constitute ownership of the stock. The purpose of this restriction is to discourage day traders and other stock speculators from buying-in the day before the ex-dividend date, and cashing-out the day after . . . and using a 15% tax rate instead of a 35% rate.

In the case of preferred stock, the holding period requirement is more than 91 days during a 181-day period, beginning 90 days before the ex-dividend date. Preferred stock is a higher class than common stock in that additional stock-purchase rights are involved. A preferred stock holder may be offered the opportunity to buy additional shares at a fixed price, within a prescribed period of time. Whether a preferred shareholder actually buys additional shares or not, his holding period for qualified dividends is 91+ days. Included in this period of time, the ex-dividend date must be one of the holding days.

Whether one owns common stock or preferred stock, the dividend rate (cents per share) is the same. That is because the total distributable earnings and profits of the corporation are divided by the total number of shares outstanding, regardless of the class of shares. The preferred stock gets priority payment and is accompanied by the offer of additional stock rights.

How Qualified Dividends Reported

Most ordinary investors do not target ex-dividend dates when acquiring, selling, or exchanging stock shares. They buy or sell with a longer view in mind. Their intention is to hold the stock for capital growth, and thus are unmindful of ex-dividend dates. As a consequence, they rely on periodic dividend statements sent to them by their payer corporations and/or their pass-through investment entities.

Once each year, every dividend payer has to report to each dividend recipient (shareholder) **and** to the IRS all dividends paid for that year. The payer reportings are made on IRS **Form 1099-DIV:** *Dividends and Distributions.* An overview of a 1099-DIV is presented in Figure 11.1. Note that the form is divided into two vertical halves. The left-hand side is general information about the payer and recipient; the right-hand side consists of about a dozen or so dollar-amount entry boxes. Only the first two of these boxes are pertinent to our discussion here. Accordingly, Box 1a is captioned: *Total ordinary dividends*; Box 1b is captioned: *Qualified dividends.* Whatever amount is entered in Box 1b is automatically included in Box 1a. There's a Copy A for the IRS, a Copy B for Recipient, and a Copy C for Payer.

Dividends and Distributions		
PAYER'S name, address, & phone no.	1a	YEAR 1099-DIV
	1b	
	2a	2b
	2c	2d
PAYER'S Tax ID / RECIPIENT'S Tax ID	3	4 ✶✶
		5
RECIPIENT'S name, address, & account no.	6	7
	8	9
✱		

✱ *Important Note: Substitute formats may be used when approved by IRS*   ✶✶ **Federal Tax Withheld**

Fig. 11.1 - General Format of IRS's Official Form 1099-DIV

Instructions on Copy B (To Recipient) say—

Box 1a. *Include this amount on line 9a of Form 1040. Also, report it on Schedule B (Form 1040).*

Box 1b. *Shows the portion of the amount in box 1a that may be eligible for the 5% or 15% capital gains rate. Report the eligible amount on line 9b, Form 1040.* [Then follow the instructions on Schedule D (Form 1040.]

Line 9a on Form 1040(for year 2004) is captioned: *Ordinary dividends. Attach Schedule B (Part II) if required.* Technically, Schedule B is required when one's total dividends from all sources exceed $1,500 for a given year. However, we suggest that, if you have more than three dividend payers (regardless of total amount), you list and identify each payer on Schedule B (Part II). Schedule B (Form 1040) is titled: **Interest and Ordinary Dividends**; its Part II is titled: *Ordinary Dividends.* The schedule will accommodate up to 21 different payers with a full separate line for each.

Line 9b on Form 1040 is captioned: *Qualified dividends (see instructions).* The instructions comprise about 700 words of text, and cover much of what we have discussed previously. The instructions include five paragraphs of exceptions to qualified dividends, and cite three numerical examples of how the holding period rules work.

What the instructions do not tell you is how to use Schedule B, Part II, to also include qualified dividends in a parallel column alongside of your postings of ordinary dividends. Our experience has been that when there are multiple payers of dividends — 5, 10, 20, or 40 — it is so easy to get confused when tallying the totals of ordinary dividends and, separately, tallying the totals of qualified dividends. Since no official separation forms are provided, you'll have to improvise on your own, including "continuation" Schedules B when there are more than 20 reportings. Confusion arises because all Form 1099-DIVs are not payer-formatted alike; *substitute* 1099-DIVs are IRS authorized. The arrangement that we suggest is depicted in Figure 11.2. Note the bold vertical line separating ordinary dividends from qualified dividends. The depiction shown becomes an excellent record — almost foolproof — when cross-checking all dividend reportings before your ultimate tax is computed.

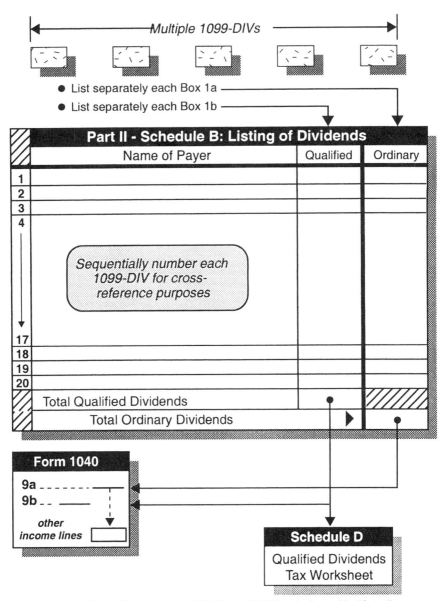

Fig. 11.2 - Use of Schedule B (1040) for Dividends from Multiple Payers

Be aware above that the qualified dividends amount is already in line **9a** (Form 1040). The line **9b** is "information" for Schedule D purposes.

Qualified Dividends Worksheet

As mentioned earlier, the term "qualified dividends" does not appear in Part I or Part II (re short/long capital transactions) of Schedule D: Capital Gains and Losses. Instead, the term appears in Part III: **Summary**, as the very last item/question thereon. Accordingly, on your 2004 Schedule D, question 22 reads:

Do you have qualified dividends on Form 1040, line 9b?

☐ *Yes. Complete Form 1040 through* **line 42**, *and then complete the Qualified Dividends and Capital Gain Tax Worksheet* [in the instructions].

☐ *No. Complete the rest of Form 1040.*

This question/instruction is telling you a fundamental procedural point. That is, with or without qualified dividends (and/or with or without net capital gain) you have to work your way through Form 1040: **U.S. Individual Income Tax Return** to line 42. This line is captioned: **Taxable Income**. One's taxable income stands alone before any applicable tax rates apply. Thus, line 42 on Form 1040 becomes the starting point for applying reduced tax rates for capital gains and qualified dividends.

We now have to tell you an unpleasant fact. The official Qualified Dividends/Capital Gain worksheet consists of 19 computational lines. Yes, 19 such lines! But don't worry; we'll address only those lines that pertain to qualified dividends.

Accordingly, lines 1 and 2 on the Qualified Dividends Worksheet read precisely as:

1. *Enter the amount from Form 1040,* **line 42** $\underline{\hspace{3cm}}$
   [Taxable income]
2. *Enter the amount from Form 1040,* **line 9b** $\underline{\hspace{3cm}}$
   [Qualified dividends]

From here on, we diagram the applicable and nonapplicable lines for you in Figure 11.3. As you can note, lines 3, 4, 5, and 6 of the official worksheet do not involve qualified dividends. So the next line of significance is line 7: *Modified taxable income.* This is your Form 1040 taxable income **reduced** by qualified dividends (and by net capital gains, if applicable). The result is ordinary taxable income at ordinary rates.

Qualified Dividends and Capital Gain Tax Worksheet	Supplements Sch. D (1040)

1. Taxable income _ 1._____
2. Qualified dividends _ _ _ _ _ _ _ _ _ _ _ _ 2._____

3.	Lines 3,4,5,& 6 relate to capital gain matters

7. Modified taxable income _ _ _ _ _ _ _ _ _ _ _ _ _ _ _ 7._____

8.	Lines 8, 9, & 10 relate to "5% threshold amounts" *(see text)*

11. Multiply line 10 by 5% (0.05) _ _ _ _ _ _ _ _ _ _ _ _ _ _ _ _ _ _ 11. _____

12.	Lines 12, 13, & 14 segregate the 15% tax rate amounts

15. Multiply line 14 by 15% (0.15) _ _ _ _ _ _ _ _ _ _ _ _ _ _ _ _ 15._____
16. Figure base tax on line 7 (use tables) _ _ _ _ _ _ _ _ _ _ _16._____
17. Add lines 11, 15, & 16 _ 17._____
18. Figure tax on line 1 (use tables) _ _ _ _ _ _ _ _ _ _ _ _ _ _ _18._____
19. Enter *smaller* of 17 or 18 here, & on Form 1040, line 43 19. [   ]

Editorial Note:	Subtract line 19 from line 18 to determine the amount of savings you derived from the lower tax rates for qualified dividends.

Fig. 11.3 - Abridged Arrangement of a Qualified Dividends Tax Worksheet

The idea is that once you get to line 7 in Figure 11.3, you immediately go to line 16. This line is officially captioned: *Figure the tax on the amount on line 7.* The effect is that line 16 becomes your base regular tax. Other computed taxes on the Qualified Dividends Tax Worksheet **add** to the base regular tax.

Two Tax Rates: 5% and 15%

One of the niceties of the Qualified Dividend (and Capital Gain) Tax Worksheet is that two separate *reduced* tax rates apply. There is a 5% tax rate for lower income taxpayers and a 15% rate for all others. The term "reduced" means relative to regular tax rates. The regular rates are graduated from 10% through 35%. Hence, the dividing line for reduced rates is the 15% regular tax bracket for ordinary income.

As of tax year 2004, the thresholds for reduced capital gain/qualified dividend tax rates are:

☐ $29,050 if single or married filing separately,

☐ $38,900 if head of household, or

☐ $58,100 if married filing jointly or qualifying widow(er).

For years subsequent to 2004, the thresholds are preprinted directly on the Tax Worksheet. We refer to these in Figure 11.3 as the "5% threshold amounts." These three amounts are preprinted on the tax worksheet at line 8.

Instructions at line 8 (in Figure 11.3) tell you to enter the **smaller** of line 1 or the amount indicated (above) corresponding to your filing status. Further instructions are preprinted at lines 9 and 10, and at lines 12, 13, and 14, for separation into the 5% and and/or 15% tax rate categories. The 5% rate amount winds up on line 11 (*Multiply line 10 by 5% (0.05)*), whereas the 15% rate amount winds up on line 15 (*Multiply line 14 by 15% (0.15)*).

The worksheet result is that the sum of lines 11, 15, and 16 (designated as line 17) become your reduced tax. For convincing you of this, you are instructed to compare the line 17 tax with the regular tax (line 18) on the line 1 amount (gross taxable income). You are instructed then to enter the **smaller of** line 17 or line 18 onto page 2 of Form 1040 at **line 43** (for year 2004). The Form 1040 line 43 reads—

Tax (see instructions). Check if any tax is from:
a. ☐ *Form(s) 8814;* *b.* ☐ *Form 4972.* ▶ _____

Although not so identified on line 43, we suggest that you add by hand a box **c.** ☐ *Schedule D Worksheet.* After a year or two, or three, have passed, should you need to recheck your tax, you'll know immediately where to start. Otherwise, you're left fumbling around redoing the tax computation that you have already done.

A "look back" at the line 43 Tax may be necessitated by an IRS inquiry, an IRS computer matching adjustment to your tax, a correction to qualified dividends payer reported, and/or a correction to a capital gain/loss transaction amount, especially one on Schedule(s) K-1. All too often, one or more Schedules K-1 come in after you have already filed your Form 1040. This forces you to amend your return — via Form 1040X — to recompute your tax based on items you may have omitted or estimated. When you have to rework a tax, it is always comforting to be reminded of what you did earlier. This is why we urge that you add to line 43 a box **c.** ☐ for "Schedule D Worksheet."

Editorial Note: Form 8814 above is titled: *Parent's Election to Report Child's Interest and Dividends.* It includes a worksheet: *Child's Qualified Dividends and Capital Gains Distributions*, which, if applicable, **adds** to your Schedule D tax. Form 4972 is titled: *Tax on Lump-Sum Distributions* from an employer's qualified pension, profit-sharing, or stock bonus plan by participants over 67 years of age. If applicable, the 20% capital gain election **adds** to your Schedule D tax.

12

COMPUTING RELATED TAX

The Term "Capital Gain" Without Any Qualification Means NET LONG-TERM Capital Gain. This Is The Cross-Netting Of Short-Term Gains & Losses With Long-Term Gains & Losses. When The Result Is Net Long-Term, REDUCED Tax Rates Apply. These Rates (As Of 2004) Are 5%, 15%, 25%, And 28% Depending On Your Taxable Income And The Nature Of Your Capital Transactions. Rarely Would The 25% Rate Apply; The 28% Rate Might Apply Occasionally. In Most Cases, Investors Would Enjoy Either The 5% Rate, The 15% Rate, Or A Combination Of Both. These Rates Apply To Qualified Dividends As Well As To Net Capital Gains.

In the chapter heading above, the term "related tax" pertains only to the reduced consequences that result from the computational processing of Schedule D (Form 1040): *Capital Gains and Losses*. The computational aspects include qualified dividends, other related forms, tax worksheets, and — yes — some old fashioned common sense.

If you really want to know about the officially detailed computations required, we refer you to the *Schedule D Tax Worksheet*. This worksheet can be found in the instructions that accompany Schedule D. We warn you, however, that the official worksheet comprises 37 computational lines. Yes, 37 lines!

Take heart; we will not go through the 37 lines one by one. Instead, we will hybridize them in other worksheet arrangements, some official, some not. Yes, we know that you have — or may have — access to tax software that could do all of the schedule D computations for you. But you would not be instructed or informed why certain computations are necessary. In this regard, we can do better than your computer software.

To overview where we are heading in this chapter, we present Figure 12.1. As we show, a "Tax Worksheet" — could be a software program — is interspersed between Form 1040 (page 1), Schedule D, and Form 1040 (page 2). Note that the Worksheet (which you keep for your records) is a supplement to Schedule D. In the "old days" (years 2003 and prior), the Worksheet was integrated into Schedule D and designated as its Part IV. The "old Part IV" (the Worksheet) now emanates from Part III.

Further note in Figure 12.1 that the worksheet starts with **line 42** of Form 1040 and ends with **line 43** thereon. Line 42 is captioned: *Taxable income*, whereas line 43 is captioned: *Tax*. Between these two lines is where all the attention lies in this chapter. To initially focus this attention, we must describe for you Schedule D, **Part III**: *Summary*.

Part III Schedule D Summary

The summary portion of Schedule D consists of **seven** instruction/question lines. The line numbers run from 16 through 22. These are the officially assigned numbers for tax year 2005. We have no idea what these line numbers will be in 2010, for example. Nevertheless, we have to use some reference year, so 2005 is it. Once we home in on a line number, we need to be very clear as to which tax form that number applies. Different forms may use the same line numbers, with vastly different instructional and computational results. So, when we cite a line number, be sure you know which tax form or schedule we are talking about.

Line 22 of Schedule D asks — *Do you have qualified dividends on Form 1040?* This is what the preceding chapter was all about. Thus, we will not pursue line 22 in this chapter.

So, let's start at the top of the Schedule D summary. The first line thereon is **line 16**. It reads precisely as—

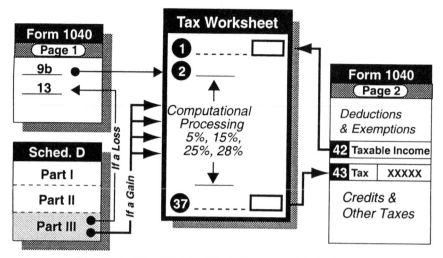

Fig. 12.1 - The "Related Tax" Aspects of Schedule D

Combine lines 7 and 15 and enter the result. If line 16 is a loss, skip lines 17 and 20, and go to line 21. If a gain, enter the gain on Form 1040, line 13, and then go to line 17 below.

Note that three sentences are cited, each of which is a separate instruction in itself. Instruction (1) is: "Combine lines 7 and 15." Instruction (2) is: "If a loss." Instruction (3) is: "If a gain." These instructions, though confusing, actually make sense. The purpose of the Schedule D summary is to establish *one* bottom-line net-net by combining two nets: one at line 7, and one at line 15.

Line 7 of Schedule D is captioned: ***Net short-term capital gain or <loss>***. Line 15 is captioned: ***Net long-term capital gain or <loss>***. When you combine the entry amounts on each of these two lines, you get either a net capital gain or a net capital loss. You get one or the other: not both. This is a net-net amount from all capital transactions for the year, including capital loss carryovers (if any) from prior year(s). This combining effort is indeed a true summary, for which Part III of Schedule D is appropriately captioned. If the combining effort of lines 7 and 15 is a net capital loss, your subsequent computational effort is much simplified. This is because of the instructions that follow.

If line 16 of Schedule D is a **loss**, you skip lines 17 through 20, and go to line 21. There you are instructed to—

*Enter here and on Form 1040, line 13, the **smaller** of—*
• The loss on line 16 or
• <$3,000>, or if married filing separately <$1,500>

Line 13 on Form 1040 is captioned: *Capital gain or <loss>.* A loss entry on this line cannot exceed <$3,000>. Having even this small a loss entry, when combined with other income entries on Form 1040, can reduce your tax modestly.

We covered net capital loss treatment in Chapter 10. With a net capital loss and having no qualified dividends, you complete the rest of Form 1040. That is, no further Schedule D computations are required. We signified this feature to you in Figure 12.1 by bypassing the Worksheet "If a loss," and going directly from Part III of Schedule D to line 13 of Form 1040.

What if you have a net capital gain instead of a loss, at line 16?

Answer: our computational participation in Part III of Schedule D increases markedly. This is fine. Isn't this what you want: net capital gain?

Pursuit of Net Capital Gain

The third instruction in line 16 says—

If a gain, enter the gain on Form 1040, line 13, and then go to line 17 below.

The line 13 of form 1040 is the same line on which you would have entered a loss, if a loss had occurred . . . instead of a gain. Recall that line 13 is captioned: *Capital gain **or** <loss>.* Also, recall earlier we emphasized that when combining lines 7 (short-term) and 15 (long-term) on Schedule D, you'd get either a net capital gain or a net capital loss. Now we are addressing net capital gain only.

With a gain in mind, what does line 17 say? It says—

*Are lines 15 and 16 **both** gains?*

☐ **Yes.** *Go to line 18*

☐ **No.** *Skip lines 18 through 21, and go to line 22.*

What is this line 17 instruction all about? It is about trying to establish the positiveness of your net long-term capital gain. Line 15 is net long-term gain, whereas line 16 is a combination of all short/long gains and losses in Parts I and II of Schedule D. If lines 15 and 16 are both gains, you have a lot of gain separation work to do. This is because all net capital gains are not taxed the same. Some are taxed at 5%, most at 15%, occasionally at 25%, and some likelihood at 28%. (Recall Figure 12.1.) This is where line 18 of Schedule D comes in.

Momentarily, let us assume that lines 15 and 16 are **not** both gains. Suppose line 15 is a loss and line 16 is gain. What does this tell you? It tells you that you have a net **short-term** capital gain. Said gain is taxed at ordinary rates (15% to 35%): not at long-term capital gain rates. So, you answer ☒ "No" to the question.

Suppose line 15 is a gain, and line 16 is a loss. What does this tell you? It tells you that you have a net capital loss. It may be a combination of short-term and long-term loss, or all one or all the other. Either way, you have a loss and answer ☒ "No" to the question at line 17.

We don't want to bog you down with "Yes/No" checkboxes. But, if you have both blank, the IRS's computer will scream.

A "No" answer to the question at line 17 directs you to line 22. This line asks—

Do you have qualified dividends on Form 1040, line 9b?
☐ *Yes* ☐ *No*

If you answer "Yes", you have a Qualified Dividends Tax Worksheet (discussed in Chapter 11) to complete. If you answer "No", you complete the rest of Form 1040 without any further use of Schedule D . . . nor any of its worksheets.

Let's go back now and answer "Yes" (instead of "No") to the question at line 17. What does a "Yes" answer entail? It entails going directly to line 18 (on Schedule D).

The 28% Rate Gain Worksheet

Line 18 of Schedule D (Form 1040) says this—

Enter the amount, if any, from line 7 of the 28% Rate Gain Worksheet [in] the instructions [to Schedule D]·

What is this instruction about? It is about totaling all collectibles gain and any section 1202 exclusion that you may have reported in Column (f), Part II, of Schedules D and D-1. Column (f) is captioned: *Gain or <loss>*. Schedule D-1 is a continuation sheet for Schedule D. The instructional inference is that, if a taxpayer/investor has any collectibles gain and/or Section 1202 exclusions, he/she is probably a sophisticated investor.

The IRS defines the term "collectibles" as including—

Works of art, rugs, antiques, metals (such as gold, silver, and platinum bullion), gems, stamps, coins, alcoholic beverages, and . . . any gain attributable to unrealized [unsold] appreciation of collectibles . . . from the sale of an [ownership] interest in a partnership, S corporation, or trust.

Section 1202 of the Tax Code allows a taxpayer to exclude up to 50% of the gain from the sale or exchange of Qualified Small Business stock held more than five years. Up to $10,000,000 (10 million) of gain can be so excluded. The Section 1202 exclusion, however, is *recaptured* at a 28% rate which, times the 50% exclusion, gives an effective capital gain rate of 14%.

Section 1(h)(4) defines the term "28-percent rate gain" as—

The excess, if any, of—
(A)   the sum of
(i)   collectibles gain; and

> (ii)   *section 1202 gain, over*
>
> (B)   *the sum of—*
>   (i)   *collectibles loss;*
>   (ii)   *the net short-term capital loss, and*
>   (iii)   *the amount of long-term capital loss carried* [forward] *to the taxable year.*

Fortunately, the IRS has prepared a quite comprehensible 7-line 28% Rate Gain Worksheet. Each line expressly identifies specific line numbers on all relevant forms and schedules from which a net collectibles gain (including any Section 1202 exclusion of gain) can be computed. If the net collectibles gain is more than zero, the line 7 instruction says—

Enter this amount on Schedule D line 18.

There are no further instructions on line 18 as to what to do. You have no choice, therefore, than to move on to line 19.

The Unrecaptured Section 1250 Worksheet

Once you have any net collectibles gain, you must read the instruction on line 19 of Schedule D. This line reads—

Enter the amount, if any, from line 18 of the Unrecaptured Section 1250 Gain Worksheet [in] *the instructions.*

You must use caution when interpreting these instructions. Line 18 of Schedule D is NOT the same as line 18 of the Unrecaptured Gain Worksheet. This instruction is telling you that there is an 18-line worksheet for determining whether you have any *unrecaptured Section 1250 gain.*

What in the world is "Unrecaptured Section 1250 gain"? To answer this, we have to get a little technical.

Section 1250 pertains to depreciable real property used in a trade or business. When such property is sold or exchanged, the transaction is reported on Form 4797: *Sales of Business Property.*

Part III of this form is captioned: *Gain from Disposition of Property under Sections . . . 1250 . . .* etc. A subcaptioned portion thereof reads—

If Section 1250 property: *If straight line depreciation was used* [at all times before sale], **enter -0-** [zero].

For years after 1975 — that's about 30 years ago — all depreciable real estate used in a trade or business had to use the straight-line method of depreciation. Real property placed in service before 1976 was allowed to claim accelerated (or additional) depreciation over and above straight line. If accelerated/additional depreciation were ever used, the excess benefit over straight line has to be recaptured as modified ordinary income: NOT as pure capital gain. The tax rate on unrecaptured Section 1250 gain is 25%.

Rare, indeed, is the investor today who acquired business real estate more than 30 years ago and who is just now selling it for the first time. Thus, it is with a high degree of certainty — over 99% — that we can urge you to disregard entirely the 18-line unrecaptured gain worksheet designated above. In other words, enter zero on line 19 of Schedule D. You could also leave line 19 blank, but we think entering "-0-" is better. This means that you have read the instruction, understood it, and the result is zero. Otherwise, leaving line 19 blank implies that the subject matter is over your head. Now, on to line 20.

Dilemma Possible at Line 20

At line 20 of Schedule D (Form 1040) for tax year 2004, you are asked—

*Are lines 18 and 19 **both** zero or blank?*

☐ ***Yes.*** *Complete Form 1040 through line 42* [taxable income], *and then complete the **Qualified Dividends and Capital Gain Tax Worksheet** [in] the instructions.*

☐   *No. Complete Form 1040 through line 42, and then complete the **Schedule D Tax Worksheet** [in] the instructions.*

***Do not** complete lines 21 and 22 below.*

Whether you answer "Yes" or "No", you, or your computer, or your tax preparer has a Worksheet to complete. The "Yes" Worksheet consists of 19 computational lines. The "No" Worksheet consists of 37 computational lines. The more the computational lines, the more the chance of error. Given the choice, one would prefer the 19-line "Yes" Worksheet to the 37-line "No" Worksheet.

But, suppose you do have some bona fide collectibles gain. In this case, line 18 would be a positive number and line 19 would be zero or blank. What do you do in this case?

Answer: It depends. It depends on the amount of collectibles gain relative to all other capital gain. It also depends on your tolerance for computer-matching by the IRS. All tax computations are routinely checked by the IRS. This is as much for your benefit as it is for the IRS's benefit. It takes about 18 months after a return is filed before the computer-matching process is complete.

Keep in mind that there's a 13% tax rate *differential* (0.13) between collectibles gain (28%) and total net capital gain (at 15%). What would happen if, say, your collectibles gain was $3,000, your total net capital gain (including collectibles) was $10,000 . . . and you left line 18 (for the 28% tax rate) blank?

Your worst case scenario is that the IRS would add about $390 [$3,000 x 0.13] to your computed tax on the "Yes" Worksheet. If you had otherwise claimed a refund, your refund would be reduced by $390 . . . but no penalty. If you computed some tax due, instead of a refund, your tax would be increased by $390. In addition, a penalty of about $100 would be applied, together with about $35 in interest. Altogether, your differential tax, penalty, and interest would be about $525 [390 + 100 + 35]. If the collectibles gain were $1,000, the differential tax, etc., would be $175. If the collectibles gain were, say, $6,000, the differential would be $875.

Or, you could plough ahead with the line 20 "Yes" Worksheet and simply add the collectibles gain differential tax to the result. In Figure 12.2, we pictorialize the dilemma (challenge?) for you.

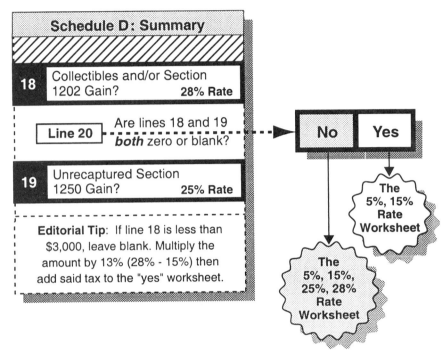

Fig. 12.2 - The Dilemma Aspect of Lines 18 and 19: Schedule D

The Capital Gain Tax Worksheet

Without your realizing it, we have already introduced you to the "Yes" Worksheet when answering the line 20 question on Schedule D. We did so in Chapter 11, at Figure 11.3 which we called the "Qualified Dividends" Tax Worksheet. At that time, because of the chapter subject focus, we skipped over all other capital gain features. This time, we skip over nothing, but we prefer to call the 'Yes" Worksheet at line 20 the *Capital Gain Tax Worksheet*. We prefer the title because the terms "capital gain" and "Schedule D" are synonymous.

Keep in mind that the Capital Gain Tax Worksheet officially applies only if lines 18 (collectibles gain) and 19 (unrecaptured gain) are **both** zero or blank. We are 99+% certain that line 19 will be zero or blank. We are not quite so certain about line 18. You may well indeed have some collectibles net gain. Even if you do, let's assume for the moment that you do not. Now what?

Line 3 of the Capital Gain Tax Worksheet asks—

Are you filing Schedule D?

☐   *Yes. Enter the **smaller** of line 15* [net long-term gain] *or line 16* [net-net capital gain] *of Schedule D, but do not enter less than -0-* [zero].

☐   *No. Enter the amount from Form 1040, line 13.*

A little explanation is in order of why the above question (re Schedule D) is framed the way it is. If you answer "Yes", the presumption is that you have a net/net long-term capital gain for the year, called: *net capital gain.* That is, your long-term capital gains exceed your short-term capital gains or exceed your capital losses, whether said losses are short-term or long-term. If this is the case, a zero entry would be totally inaccurate. It would throw off the IRS's computer cross-check processing, and trigger an error in your computations. Any computer-triggered error is always a cause for closer examination of your return.

If you answer "No" to line 3 on the Tax Worksheet, the presumption is that you have no net capital gain. Instead, the presumption is that you have capital gain distributions from one or more mutual funds. In such case, the completion of Schedule D is not required. On this point, the preprinted instructions at line 13 of Form 1040 say—

Attach Schedule D if required. If not required, check here ☐

The "check here" instructions to Form 1040 do not require a Schedule D if—

*The only amounts you have to report on Schedule D are capital gain distributions on Form(s) 1099-DIV, **box 2a**, or on substitute forms.*

Box 2a on Form 1099-DIV (Dividends and Distributions) is captioned: *Total capital gain distributions.* The term "total" includes (b) unrecaptured Section 1250 gain, and (d) collectibles gain. Capital gain distributions are made almost exclusively by mutual funds. When so designated and assigned to shareholders, the distributions are automatically treated as net (long-term) capital gain. That is, there are no holding-period requirements to be met. This automatic feature alone (capital gain treatment) makes mutual funds very popular with ordinary investors.

The Form 4952 Election

The next instruction of significance on the Capital Gain Tax Worksheet is its line 5. At this line, you are asked—

*If you are claiming investment interest expense on **Form 4952**, enter the amount from **line 4g** of that form. Otherwise, enter -0- [zero].*

Line 4g of Form 4952: ***Investment Interest Expense Deduction***, has no official caption. It is simply an instruction which says—

*Enter the amounts from lines 4b [qualified dividends] and 4e [net capital gain] **that you elect to include** in investment income. [Emphasis added.]*

Investment interest expense is interest paid on borrowed money to carry on your investment objectives. You get no deduction for any excess investment interest expense that exceeds your investment income. Form 4952 allows you to offset excess investment interest with part or all of your net capital gain (including qualified dividends). This gives you a direct deduction against other sources of taxable income and permits you to bypass some or all of the Capital Gain Tax Worksheet.

The Form 4952 **elected** amount is subtracted from your total net capital gain, which includes qualified dividends, to arrive at a residual net capital gain. This becomes line 6 on the Tax Worksheet. When subtracting line 6 from line 1 (ordinary taxable income) you get a *modified* taxable income: line 7. The tax on this line becomes your foundation for capital gains tax add-ons.

We put the above together for you in the line sequence below, and functionalize them for you in Figure 12.3. That is, the first seven lines of the Capital Gain Tax Worksheet are—

1. Ordinary taxable income $_____
   — Form 1040, line 42
2. Qualified dividends   _____
   — Form 1040, line 9b
3. Net capital gain   _____
   — See text earlier
4. ADD lines 2 and 3   _____
   — Combined tax treatment
5. Form 4952 election   <   >
   — See text above
6. SUBTRACT line 5 from line 4   _____
   — Residual capital gain
7. SUBTRACT line 6 from line 1 $_____
   — Modified taxable income

In Figure 12.3, we tip you off to a little computational secret. Your tax after capital gain treatment will be somewhere between the tax on line 1 and the tax on line 7. The tax on line 1 represents the ordinary tax you would pay **without** any capital gain tax rate benefits. The tax on line 7 represents the least amount of tax applicable after subtracting all residual capital gain from line 1. Thus, you could detour for a moment and look up the corresponding tax (to lines 1 and 7) in the Tax Table or Tax Computation Worksheet (whichever applies). Eventually, your Schedule D tax would be the sum of line 7, plus any 5% rate on capital gains, plus the 15% rate on capital gains, plus the 28% rate on collectibles gain (if any).

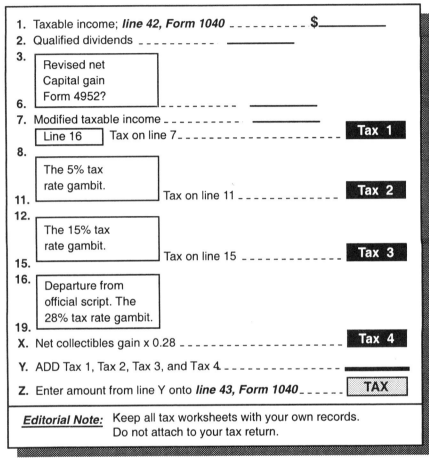

Fig. 12.3 - Functionalized Capital Gain Tax Worksheet

How the 5% Tax Rate Works

The Capital Gain Tax Worksheet allocates lines 8, 9, 10, and 11 to the 5% tax rate computational process. It is instructive to review each of these lines as they appear on the official worksheet.

So, right off, line 8 says—

*Enter the **smaller** of:*
- *The amount on line 1, or* }
- *$29,050 if single or married filing separately,* }
- *$38,900 if head of household,* }
- *$58,100 if married filing jointly or qualifying* } _____
  widow(er) }

Line 8, therefore, is simply a *smaller of* entry: line 1 or a designated filing-status threshold. Shortly below, we'll go through a 3-case example where line 1 is $50,000; $85,000; and $150,000. Keep in mind that line 1 is your ordinary taxable income, without any capital gain tax rate benefit. Meanwhile, on to line 9 (of the Capital Gain Tax Worksheet). [***Caution***: Be aware that we are focusing here on IRS *Worksheet* line numbers: **not** those on Schedule D.]

Line 9 on the Worksheet asks—

Is the amount on line 7 equal to or more than the amount on line 8?

☐ *Yes. Skip lines 9 through 11; go to line* }
  12 and check the "No" box [at line 12]. }
                                           } _____
                                           }
☐ *No. Enter the amount from line 7.* }

If line 7 is equal to or greater than line 8, check the "Yes" box. Thereupon, the 5% capital gain tax rate would not apply. It is only when line 7 is less than line 8 — the "No" box — that the 5% rate is valid. Line 8, as presented above, comprises the filing status thresholds below which the 5% rate is intended. In just a moment, we'll exemplify numerically what we mean.

Lines 10 and 11 on the Capital Gain Tax Worksheet are purely arithmetic. Line 10 is a subtraction; line 11 is a multiplication. They read in full as—

10. *Subtract line 9 from line 8* _____
11. *Multiply line 10 by 5% (0.05)* _____

Numerical Examples at 5%

Let us suppose that you are married filing a joint return for year 2004. This means that for the 5% capital gains tax rate to apply, the applicable threshold amount is $58,100. Suppose now that your line 1 amount (ordinary taxable income from Form 1040) is: Case A — $50,000; Case B — $85,000; and Case C — $150,000. Let us further suppose that the line 6 applicable capital gains amount (at this point) is $20,000 for all three cases. What is the amount of gain (at line 10) subject to the 5% tax rate, and what is the amount of that tax (at line 11)?

Answer: We list the computations as follows:

	Case A	Case B	Case C
Line 1 (assumed)	$50,000	$85,000	$150,000
Line 6 (assumed)	20,000	20,000	20,000
Line 7 (subtract 6 from 1)	30,000	65,000	130,000
Line 8 (smaller of 1 or threshold)	50,000	58,100	58,100
Line 9 (7 equal to or more than 8)	No	Yes	Yes
	30,000	skip	skip
Line 10 (subtract 9 from 8)	20,000	skip	skip
Line 11 (line 10 x 0.05)	$ 1,000	-0-	-0-

It is obvious from the numbers assumed that Case A enjoys a 5% capital gain tax rate, whereas Cases B and C do not. Furthermore, since the line 6 amount and the line 10 amount are the same ($20,000), there is no excess capital gain to which the 15% tax rate could apply. Thus, you can push the 5% rate to as high as the applicable threshold for your filing status.

Suppose now for Case A, we assume that line 1 is $58,100 (the 5% threshold amount for 2004) instead of $50,000. There are no other changes to Case A. Using the line sequences and data above, what happens?

Line 7 becomes $38,100 [58,100 – 20,000]; line 8 becomes $58,100 (the same as line 1); line 9 becomes $38,100 (the same as line 7); and line 10 becomes $20,000 [58,100 – 38,100]. Line 12 is thereby unchanged: $1,000 (20,000 x 0.05).

There is an important corollary here. If line 1 (your ordinary taxable income) is *equal to or less than* the 5% tax rate threshold amount (for your Form 1040 filing status), your total capital gains tax rate is 5%.

Let us drop case A and move to Cases B and C. Both have line 1 amounts which exceed the 5% tax rate threshold of $58,100 for married filing jointly.

Numerical Examples at 15%

Let us tweak the Case B and Case C amounts just a bit. Instead of an applicable capital gain of $20,000, suppose it is $35,000. Now, what happens?

Using the line sequences above, we have—

	Case B	Case C
Line 1	$85,000	$150,000
Line 6	35,000	35,000
Line 7	50,000	115,000
Line 8	58,100	58,100
Line 9	No	Yes
	50,000	skip
Line 10	8,100	skip
Line 11 (10 x 0.05)	405	-0-

Thus, in Case B, it is obvious that a small portion of the $35,000 capital gain amount ($8,100) will get a 5% tax rate benefit. The consequent reduced applicable capital gain amount becomes $26,900 [35,000 – 8.100]. Intuition should tell you that, absent any collectibles gain, the $26,900 should be subject to the 15% tax rate. Indeed it is, because we are assuming for the moment there is no collectibles gain. Hence, the 15% tax would be $4,035 [26,900 x 0.15].

The point that we are making is that, in a case like B, it is possible to have both a 5% tax rate component **and** a 15% tax rate component.

How does the Capital Gain Tax Worksheet proceed?

It proceeds with lines 12, 13, 14, and 15.

Line 12 asks—

Are the amounts on lines 6 and 10 the same?

☐   *Yes. Skip lines 12 through 15: go to line 16.*   }
                                                        } _____
☐   *No. Enter the **smaller** of line 1 or line 6.*   }

From the above Case B and Case C amounts, a "No" answer is indicated. For Case A, a "Yes" would be indicated. A "yes" to line 12 means that no 15% tax rate applies.

The next three lines read precisely as—

13.   Enter the amount from line 10 (if line 10 is
          blank, enter -0-)   _____
14.   Subtract line 13 from line 12   _____
15.   Multiply line 14 by 15% (0.15)   _____

Continuing with the Case B and Case C line sequences, we have as follows:

	Case B	Case C
	No	No
Line 12 (line 6 smaller)	35,000	35,000
Line 13 (line 10 or zero)	8,100	-0-
Line 14 (13 from 12)	26,900	35,000
Line 15 (14 x 0.15)	4,035	5,250

Isn't line 15 the Case B intuitive amount that we speculated above? Keep this intuitive premise in mind as we go to Case C with collectibles gain. We intend to use intuitive common sense to simplify and shortcut what otherwise is a very complex computational process (whether by worksheet or software).

What if Collectibles Gain?

As pointed out previously, collectibles gain is taxed at a 28% rate instead of 15%. Where collectibles gain, including the Section 1202 qualified small business exclusion, if any, is involved, the worksheet computational process shifts to ultra-sophistication. Instead of the 19-line Capital Gains tax Worksheet that we have been using, a 37-line *Schedule D Tax Worksheet* comes into play. What does the Schedule D Tax Worksheet actually do?

Answer: It "baskets" the total net capital gain for the year into four tax rate categories: 5%, 15%, 25%, and 28%. As described earlier, the 25% rate applies only to depreciable real property held more than 30 years before being sold. As such, the 25% rate gain is highly unlikely to be an issue. We think it is 99+% unlikely.

Where there is collectibles gain (with or without the 50% Section 1202 exclusion), higher income taxpayers are likely to be involved. This is why we postulated Case C above. At the Case C income level of $150,000, there is little or no likelihood that a 5% tax rate would apply. So, now we are down to essentially two capital gain tax rates: 15% and 28%.

To address the 28% issue, let's assume that the total capital gain for Case C is $50,000 (instead of $35,000). The $15,000 additional amount is collectibles gain.

The simplest (common sense) way to address the 28% rate situation is to multiply the $15,000 of collectibles gain by 28%. The result would be $4,200 [15,000 x 0.28].

To this $4,200 amount, we add the 15% on $35,000 [$50,000 total capital gain minus the $15,000 of collectibles gain]. The 15% rate amount comes to $5,250 [35,000 x 0.15]. The two rate amounts (15% and 28%), when combined, total $9,450 [5,250 + 4,200]. That's on $50,000 of total capital gain.

For Case C, we have line 1 (ordinary taxable income) at $150,000 and line 6 (residual capital gain) at $50,000. The line 7 (modified taxable income) becomes $100,000 [150,000 – 50,000]. Using the year 2004 regular tax computation worksheet *without* capital gain considerations, the ordinary tax on $100,000 is

$18,475 (married filing jointly). What is the total tax (at this point) on the Case C amount?

It is a combination of—

(a)	tax on the line 7 $100,000 amount	$18,475
(b)	*plus* tax on the 15% rate $35,000 amount	5,250
(c)	*plus* tax on the 28% rate $15,000 amount	4,200
(d)	combined tax on $150,000............................	$27,925

For comparison purposes, the ordinary tax on the line 1 $150,000 amount would be $31,960

Thus, the tax saving for Case C, by virtue of the 15% and 28% capital gain rates, is $4,035 [31,960 – 27,925]. If there were no collectibles gain, the 28% rate would not apply. The 15% rate on $50,000 of capital gain would be $7,500 [50,000 x 0.15]. This would add another $1,950 [(5,250 + 4,200) – 7,500] to your Case C savings. See how simple things could be?

Summary of Schedule D Summary

Our premise is that you have completed all applicable portions of Part I (short-term) and Part II (long-term) of Schedule D (1040) that are applicable to your capital transactions for the year. You are at the first line (line 16) of Part III (Summary) and have carefully read the instructions thereon. You do not have a net capital loss; you have a net capital gain. Having a loss at this point means that you enter the **smaller of** the line 16 loss or <$3,000> on page 1 of form 1040. You then complete Form 1040 without any further reference to Schedule D.

Having a net capital gain on line 16 of Schedule D means that you could be exposed to—

1. A 28% Rate Gain Worksheet (of **7** computational lines);

2. An Unrecaptured Section 1250 Gain Worksheet (of **18** computational lines);

3. A Qualified Dividends and Capital Gain Tax Worksheet (of **19** computational lines); and/or

4. A Schedule D Tax Worksheet (of **37** computational lines).

Altogether, 81 (7 + 18 + 19 + 37) computational lines are potentially applicable. With a little common sense and some tolerance for imperfection, we can trim these worksheets down to just six steps! Here goes . . .

Step 1. Establish your total applicable capital gain. This is line 16 of Schedule D, *plus* your qualified dividends, *minus* your elected amounts on Form 4952: capital gain offsets against investment interest expense.

Step 2. Subtract step 1 from your taxable income shown on line 42 of Form 1040. This becomes your "modified" (reduced by capital gains) taxable income. Determine the tax on this amount (via Tax tables, etc.) and set the result aside as **Tax 1**.

Step 3. If your taxable income (line 42, Form 1040) is equal to or **less than** the 5% rate thresholds (cited earlier), then all of your step 1 capital gain is taxed at 5%. Multiply and set the result aside as **Tax 2**.

Step 4. Cull through **column (f)** [Gain or <loss>] of Part II of Schedules D and D-1 and strip out all collectibles gain and reverse any Section 1202 exclusions claimed. If net positive, multiply by 28% and set the result aside as **Tax 3**.

Step 5. Subtract your 5% rate capital gain (in step 3) **plus** your 28% rate capital gain (in step 4) from step 1. This amount becomes your residual (to be taxed) capital gain. *Assume* this is all taxable at 15%. Multiply and set the result aside as **Tax 4**.

Step 6. Add together Tax 1, Tax 2, Tax 3, and Tax 4. Enter the total on **line 43** of Form 1040 (labeled: ***Tax***). Then follow the instructions on Form 1040 for other taxes and credits.

Are there any imperfections in the abbreviated sequence above? You bet there are. At step 4, if you have more than three collectibles and Section 1202 transactions, you are advised to do the 7-step worksheet in the Schedule D instructions. Step 5 could produce some slight overtaxation should there be any 5% rate capital gain in your residual capital gain amount at 15%.

What should you do about these tax imperfections?

Answer: Let the IRS correct you. Whether your entry on line 43 Form 1040 is high, low, or perfect, the IRS will run all of your Schedule D and 1099-DIV payer reportings through its Big Computer software programs. It does this for everyone . . . even those who use sophisticated Schedule D computer software. If you've made an error, you'll receive an official **CP 2000 Notice**. This Notice will show less refund, more refund, or more tax to pay. If more tax to pay, there'll be no penalty (usually), but interest will be added. So, do take comfort in *all* that we have presented (in this chapter or in others). You will not go to jail if you've made an honest error.

ABOUT THE AUTHOR

Holmes F. Crouch

Born on a small farm in southern Maryland, Holmes was graduated from the U.S. Coast Guard Academy with a Bachelor's Degree in Marine Engineering. While serving on active duty, he wrote many technical articles on maritime matters. After attaining the rank of Lieutenant Commander, he resigned to pursue a career as a nuclear engineer.

Continuing his education, he earned a Master's Degree in Nuclear Engineering from the University of California. He also authored two books on nuclear propulsion. As a result of the tax write-offs associated with writing these books, the IRS audited his returns. The IRS's handling of the audit procedure so annoyed Holmes that he undertook to become as knowledgeable as possible regarding tax procedures. He became a licensed private Tax Practitioner by passing an examination administered by the IRS. Having attained this credential, he started his own tax preparation and counseling business in 1972.

In the early years of his tax practice, he was a regular talk-show guest on San Francisco's KGO Radio responding to hundreds of phone-in tax questions from listeners. He was a much sought-after guest speaker at many business seminars and taxpayer meetings. He also provided counseling on special tax problems, such as divorce matters, property exchanges, timber harvesting, mining ventures, animal breeding, independent contractors, selling businesses, and offices-at-home. Over the past 25 years, he has prepared well over 10,000 tax returns for individuals, estates, trusts, and small businesses (in partnership and corporate form).

During the tax season of January through April, he prepares returns in a unique manner. During a single meeting, he completes the return . . . *on the spot!* The client leaves with his return signed, sealed, and in a stamped envelope. His unique approach to preparing returns and his personal interest in his clients' tax affairs have honed his professional proficiency. His expertise extends through itemized deductions, computer-matching of income sources, capital gains and losses, business expenses and cost of goods, residential rental expenses, limited and general partnership activities, closely-held corporations, to family farms and ranches.

He remembers spending 12 straight hours completing a doctor's complex return. The next year, the doctor, having moved away, utilized a large accounting firm to prepare his return. Their accountant was so impressed by the manner in which the prior return was prepared that he recommended the doctor travel the 500 miles each year to have Holmes continue doing it.

He recalls preparing a return for an unemployed welder, for which he charged no fee. Two years later the welder came back and had his return prepared. He paid the regular fee . . . and then added a $300 tip.

During the off season, he represents clients at IRS audits and appeals. In one case a shoe salesman's audit was scheduled to last three hours. However, after examining Holmes' documentation it was concluded in 15 minutes with "no change" to his return. In another instance he went to an audit of a custom jeweler that the IRS dragged out for more than six hours. But, supported by Holmes' documentation, the client's return was accepted by the IRS with "no change."

Then there was the audit of a language translator that lasted two full days. The auditor scrutinized more than $1.25 million in gross receipts, all direct costs, and operating expenses. Even though all expensed items were documented and verified, the auditor decided that more than $23,000 of expenses ought to be listed as capital items for depreciation instead. If this had been enforced it would have resulted in a significant additional amount of tax. Holmes strongly disagreed and after many hours explanation got the amount reduced by more than 60% on behalf of his client.

He has dealt extensively with gift, death and trust tax returns. These preparations have involved him in the tax aspects of wills, estate planning, trustee duties, probate, marital and charitable bequests, gift and death exemptions, and property titling.

Although not an attorney, he prepares Petitions to the U.S. Tax Court for clients. He details the IRS errors and taxpayer facts by citing pertinent sections of tax law and regulations. In a recent case involving an attorney's ex-spouse, the IRS asserted a tax deficiency of $155,000. On behalf of his client, he petitioned the Tax Court and within six months the IRS conceded the case.

Over the years, Holmes has observed that the IRS is not the industrious, impartial, and competent federal agency that its official public imaging would have us believe.

He found that, at times, under the slightest pretext, the IRS has interpreted against a taxpayer in order to assess maximum penalties, and may even delay pending matters so as to increase interest due on additional taxes. He has confronted the IRS in his own behalf on five separate occasions, going before the U.S. Claims Court, U.S. District Court, and U.S. Tax Court. These were court actions that tested specific sections of the Internal Revenue Code which he found ambiguous, inequitable, and abusively interpreted by the IRS.

Disturbed by the conduct of the IRS and by the general lack of tax knowledge by most individuals, he began an innovative series of taxpayer-oriented Federal tax guides. To fulfill this need, he undertook the writing of a series of guidebooks that provide in-depth knowledge on one tax subject at a time. He focuses on subjects that plague taxpayers all throughout the year. Hence, his formulation of the "Allyear" Tax Guide series.

The author is indebted to his wife, Irma Jean, and daughter, Barbara MacRae, for the word processing and computer graphics that turn his experiences into the reality of these publications. Holmes welcomes comments, questions, and suggestions from his readers. He can be contacted in California at (408) 867-2628, or by writing to the publisher's address.

ALLYEAR Tax Guides
by Holmes F. Crouch

For information about the above titles, contact
Holmes F. Crouch

Allyear Tax Guides
Phone: (408) 867-2628   Fax: (408) 867-6466